I Don't Do That Anymore

Breaking Free from Addiction

I Don't Do That Anymore

Breaking Free from Addiction

Joey McCollum

THE
McCOLLUM
GROUP

The McCollum Group

This book shares the author's personal experiences and reflections on recovery and growth. It is not a substitute for professional advice or treatment. The author is not a medical, legal, or mental health professional, and the information here is offered for educational and inspirational purposes only. Each person's situation is unique—use what helps, set aside what doesn't, and always seek qualified help when needed. The author and publisher disclaim any liability for the use or misuse of the information contained herein.

ISBN-13: 978-1-969835-02-5 (paperback)

Dedicated to the three most important women in my life: Emily, Brandy & Debbie.

For Emily—my reason to heal.
May you always know it's never too late to change.
Keep God first.
Choose truth.
Live with courage.
Lead with love.
And never forget:
My love for you has no end.

You are my heart
You are my world
You'll always be
Daddy's girl

-January 21, 2015

To my wife, Brandy—thank you for standing beside me in the hardest moments and believing in the man I could become, even when I couldn't see him myself. Your strength, patience, and love are pillars in my life. You've been my steady through every storm—fierce, loyal, and all-in. I'm better because of you. I love you more than words will ever capture.

To my mom, Debbie—thank you for introducing me to Jesus early on. You were the first to show me what faith looked like, and those roots stayed with me, even when I drifted. Thank you for loving me through every season, through every mistake. You never gave up on me, no matter how far I fell, and I am forever grateful for that.

Contents

Foreword

Joey McCollum is one of a kind. What you'll experience in these pages isn't just a story—it's a testimony. It's a raw, unfiltered look at the human spirit when it's tested, broken, and then rebuilt stronger than ever.

Joey opens up about one of the most life-changing seasons anyone can go through: his battle with addiction. But what sets him apart is not just *what* he overcame—it's *how* he did it. He didn't hide behind pride or pretense. He leaned into vulnerability, faced the mirror, and did the hard internal work that most people run from.

Through his storytelling, Joey doesn't just recount events—he invites us into transformation. He shares real tools, real pain, and real hope. His insights don't come from theory; they come from the trenches. And that's why they hit so deep.

Joey is more than a survivor—he's a guide for anyone searching for freedom, purpose, or redemption. His courage reminds us that no matter how far we fall, grace and grit can always lead us home.

Joey McCollum is a true treasure—and this book is proof that his life's purpose is to help others find theirs. Protect this man (he's a National treasure). Cherish his words. They just might change your life.

— Alex Molden

Former NFL'er (8-years), Keynote Speaker, Author (2x), Leadership Consultant, and Personal Development Coach

Introduction: Why I Named This Book *I Don't Do That Anymore*

There was a time in my life when those five words didn't exist in my vocabulary. Back then, I didn't even think about changing. I was too busy doing what I always did.

Drinking. Numbing. Running.

I wasn't living intentionally. I was reacting.

Running from feelings I didn't want to deal with. It didn't feel like self-destruction. It just felt normal.

The first time I said, *"I don't do that anymore,"* I said it aloud after getting a sudden urge to grab a pinch of chewing tobacco. There was no one else around. Just me and my pickup truck, driving down a country road in the middle of Yamhill County, Oregon. It was the only thing standing between me and a life that I decided I wanted.

I didn't know how powerful those words would become in my life. I just knew I needed something, anything, to get me through the moment. Because that's where change actually happens. Not in months. Not in years. In moments. One day, one minute, one second at a time.

My first real moment came three years ago, standing in the wreckage of what alcohol had done to my life. I wasn't drinking to celebrate anymore. I was drinking to forget. To escape. To survive.

The truth hit harder than I expected: I wasn't just tired. I was broken. I was ashamed. I was physically sick. I was out of options other than to put down the drink. My doctor also told me I would die if I didn't stop drinking.

So I quit.

It wasn't clean. It wasn't pretty. It was gritty, extremely uncomfortable, and messy. But it was what needed to be done, and it opened the door to everything else.

About two years later, it was chewing tobacco. Another thing I had leaned on without even questioning it. I told myself it wasn't a big deal, at least not compared to alcohol. But the truth was, it owned me the same way.

I didn't want to be mostly free. I wanted to be all in. To be completely free.

So I quit again.

This time, when the cravings hit, I found myself saying something simple out loud: *"I don't do that anymore."*

No debate.

No bargaining.
Just truth.

I eliminated choice. There was no choosing yes or no. The only choice I had was to not pick it up.

And it worked. It got me through the most dangerous part, the first seven seconds of the craving. That's the window where most people break. But that one line reminded me: I had already decided. I didn't need to think about it again.

I kept saying it. Every time the old life tried to call me back, I answered the same way. Until it wasn't just something I said, it became something I lived.

I don't do that anymore became more than a phrase

It became a boundary.
A mindset.
A new identity.

Because the truth is, I wasn't just quitting substances. I was quitting the patterns that kept me stuck.

I was done running from my problems.
I was done running from my feelings.
I was done reaching for something outside of me every time life got heavy inside of me.

I finally realized: The things I thought were helping me survive were actually the things keeping me trapped.

That's when it clicked: This wasn't just about quitting drinking. It wasn't just about quitting chewing.

It wasn't even just about addiction.
It was about leaving behind anything that didn't serve the life I was trying to build.
The addictions.
The excuses.
The ways I ran from my feelings.
The lies I told myself.
The reacting to life instead of living intentionally.
It was about figuring out who I was.

People hear the title and they smile or nod and say, "That's powerful."

It is, but not because it sounds good.

It's powerful because it's simple.

In the hardest moments five words can help see you through.

It was only alcohol for me, no other drugs or substances, but it found its way into every part of my life. Eventually, I realized:

I can't coach people through addiction and recovery if I'm still secretly chained to my own.

I can't talk about freedom if I'm still hiding behind habits.

I can't ask people to trust me if I'm not living the same truth I'm offering them.

So I made a decision.
I chose alignment.
I chose freedom over image.
I chose to live a life that matched the message I was sharing.

That's what this book is about.

It's not about being perfect.
It's not about pretending you're fine when you're falling apart inside.
It's not just about quitting drinking or chewing or anything else you've used to survive.
It's about getting honest about the stuff that's been weighing you down, and deciding you're done carrying it.
It's about facing the truth you've been running from.
It's about refusing to settle for a life that's smaller than the one you were made for.
It's about integrity.
It's about ownership.
It's about freedom that doesn't come cheap, but changes everything.

This is about fighting for the life you were meant to live.

It's about standing your ground when everything in you wants to run.

It's about being able to look yourself in the eye and mean it when you say,

"I don't do that anymore."

Top Things People Don't Do Anymore:

- I don't drink alcohol anymore.
- I don't use nicotine anymore.
- I don't use drugs anymore.
- I don't lie to myself anymore.
- I don't numb my feelings anymore.
- I don't make excuses for my mistakes anymore.
- I don't run from the hard conversations anymore.
- I don't stay stuck in shame anymore.
- I don't chase people's approval anymore.
- I don't live like I'm powerless anymore.

Now it's your turn. What don't *you* do anymore?

(Write your own "I don't" statements below. Keep it honest. Keep it simple. This is your truth. And hey—it's totally okay to use some of mine if they speak to you.)

- I don't _____
- I don't _____
- I don't _____
- I don't _____
- I don't _____

This is where your story starts.

Let's find out who you're becoming.

Chapter 1: My Story

I came from a long line of alcoholics. It ran deep in my family, generation after generation. I saw the damage it could do from a young age. The negative effects it could have on people's lives and how it could tear families apart. Because of that, and because I was focused on sports, drinking was never an option for me growing up. Not in high school, not during those years when I was grinding to make something of myself on the court and on the field.

I was too committed to the game. I knew alcohol would only get in the way. My body was my tool, my job, my identity, and I protected it. There was no way I was putting any of that kind of garbage in it.

In high school, I was the guy everyone knew. I played football and basketball, and I was good at them both. All-State good, in both sports. I was on the front page of the local paper more times than I could count. My name was commonly being talked about on the local news. My highlights played on repeat in living rooms, and people around town would point me out like I was already somebody.

That kind of attention does something to you. It wraps itself around your identity until you can't tell where the performance ends and the person begins. My self-worth, my future, my entire sense of who I was felt tied to that success.

Friday nights under the lights weren't just football games, they were stages. And on those stages, I felt like a star. That feeling of walking onto the field and hearing the roar of the crowd, seeing the stadium lights stretch across the night sky like a halo, it lit me up.

I didn't know it at the time, but I was being shaped by that spotlight. Molded by the cheers. Carved by the expectations. And I loved it. Every second of it.

It wasn't just about the wins or the personal accolades. It was about being seen. Being valued. Being somebody. That attention became addictive. It wasn't just part of my story, it became a part of me.

So when I got recruited to play football at the University of Oregon, it felt like the natural next chapter in a story that had already been written. The dream was unfolding exactly how it was supposed to, and it was like the world was confirming, Yes, you're on the path. You've made it. Keep going.

But glory fades fast. Its shine doesn't light the next field, and it absolutely doesn't guarantee your future.

My high school accolades didn't carry me into college success. They don't mean much when you walk into a locker room full of guys who were all the best in their hometowns, too. Everyone was fast. Everyone was strong. Everyone had stories of Friday night lights and newspaper clippings. The playing field had leveled out, and I was no longer the top dog. I was just another name on the roster.

And instead of meeting that moment with humility and hunger, I brought an ego. I walked in with my chin high, chest out, thinking, I belong here. I've earned this.

What I should've thought was, I need to earn this again, every day. Every practice. Every rep.

But I didn't. That attitude, that entitlement, set the tone for everything that followed. I expected the game to keep giving. I thought it owed me something. When things didn't click immediately, I got frustrated. I felt overlooked. Underappreciated.

Instead of doubling down and grinding harder, I got in my own way. I let bitterness creep in. I focused on what I wasn't getting instead of what I needed to give. Eventually, I left the school I had dreamed of playing for since I was a little boy. Opportunity and a dream lived out, wasted.

I transferred to Montana State, hoping for a reset. A second chance. I accepted a scholarship to play running back, thinking a smaller program might mean more opportunity. Maybe even redemption.

But the National Collegiate Athletic Association (NCAA) had other plans. I was ruled ineligible due to transfer rules. And to make things worse, I didn't click with the coaching staff. The environment felt cold to me. Distant. And the fire in me, the one that used to burn hot, was starting to flicker.

That's when it started.

Around that time, after the eligibility ruling, I felt it all slipping away. The dream. The identity. The future I'd wrapped my whole life around. That's when I started drinking. I was 20 years old, and I had just watched the life I'd built crumble right in front of me. I didn't know how to grieve it. I didn't know how to talk about it.

So I reached for something that could quiet the noise in my head. Something that would numb the ache. Alcohol became that thing. What started as an escape quickly became a habit. And from that point forward, it was always in the background, waiting for me whenever I didn't want to face the truth.

Then came the knee injury. During spring ball, I tore it up bad. Surgery was inevitable. I came home for the procedure, and during recovery, the question I'd been avoiding for months finally caught up with me:

Was it time to walk away?

The answer came faster than I expected. I was done. Just like that, the sport that had defined me, carried me, celebrated me, was now behind me. Gone. And with it went the structure. The spotlight. The sense of purpose. For a while, I told myself I was okay with it. I thought I had moved on. I thought I was fine.

But I wasn't.

I started coaching high school football at my alma mater. For thirteen seasons, I poured my energy into that role. I gave everything I had to those kids, my knowledge, my passion, my discipline, my heart.

It felt good to be back on the field, even if I wasn't playing. To share what I'd learned, to pass it down. In many ways, it felt like redemption. But deep down, it still wasn't the same.

Around the same time my coaching career began, I also started working for my father at the company he started in 1980. My brother joined in too, and the three of us were fortunate enough to spend several years working side by side and growing the company into a 5-location operation with almost 100 employees total.

In 2012, I became an owner. We were proud of the work we were doing on a day-to-day basis. But inside, something was missing. There was a dullness inside of me that I couldn't name. A kind of quiet sadness that followed me from room to room. It wasn't loud, but it was constant.

I have never grieved the loss of the athlete I used to be. I am not sure I ever will either. But, I didn't realize how much of my identity was tethered to the game. To the affirmation. To the applause. Without it, I felt hollow. And in that emptiness, I found something that filled the silence: alcohol.

Drinking became my new arena. And just like before, I got good at it. I knew how to entertain. How to make people laugh. How to command a room. I became the life of the party. The funny one. The loud one. And it felt familiar. Like I had found a new version of that old spotlight.

But it wasn't joy. It was pain, disguised. I drank to forget. It allowed me to not face the hard truths of my past. It was a way of running away from it all.

And then came the day that changed everything.

It started on a golf course, of all places. I felt something off in my stomach, like a washing machine churning inside me. Something wasn't right. I went to the doctor. They ran tests and did bloodwork, then sent me to a liver specialist.

The liver specialist walked in holding my chart. His voice was calm, but there was no softness in it. No hesitation. Just a fact.

"If you don't quit drinking, you will die." He locked eyes with me as if to make sure I understood. And I did.

Right then, in that cold and unwelcoming room, I felt it in my bones, this wasn't a warning I could ignore. This was real. My chest tightened. My mind raced. The lump in my throat made it hard to swallow.

And then, clear as day, I saw my daughter. Years from now. Standing in a white dress. A beautiful wedding. Guests filling the seats. Music playing. Flowers lining the aisle.

But I wasn't there.

An empty chair, next to her mother, where her father should've been. Someone else walking her down the aisle. A moment that should've been mine, but was taken by a bottle.

Then another image danced through my head. One I'd never considered before. A tiny hand wrapping around my daughter's finger. My first grandchild. A life I would never meet. A legacy I wouldn't get to shape.

My throat went dry. My hands started shaking, but not from withdrawal. From fear. For the first time in my life, I wasn't afraid of living without alcohol. I was afraid of dying because of it.

That was the moment everything shifted.

I made the decision right there: I will never drink again. I haven't. And I won't. That was July 25th, 2022. I was 40 years old.

I didn't know you could die from alcohol withdrawals, though. Guess I should have paid more attention in school all those years ago. Nonetheless, I found myself in the fetal position, rocking uncontrollably back and forth on the floor of my master bedroom.

Luckily for me, my wife came home just in time to get me up, into the car, and off to the emergency room. I'm lucky and thankful that she did; otherwise, they said I likely would have died.

They admitted me immediately for medical detox. And that's where I hit rock bottom. It was lying in that hospital bed, no longer shaking from withdrawal because I was so heavily medicated, tubes in my arms, nurses checking my vitals every few hours. It was the weight of knowing how far I had fallen.

I felt like I had let everyone down. My family and loved ones. My friends. And most of all, myself.

The guilt was suffocating. But I wasn't alone. I was surrounded by the people who mattered most in my life. My family. My closest friends. The ones who never gave up on me. They came with love. With support. With grace. Without judgement.

And above all of them, above all of it, was God. Even in the moments when I felt most lost, most broken, most ashamed, He never left my side. Not once.

Then came a moment I will never forget. My life coach visited me in the hospital. I was crying, completely broken, and he didn't try to fix anything. He just looked at me and said: "Remember this moment." Three simple words, but they cut straight through me. Remember this moment. The pain. The truth. The brokenness.

That was my rock bottom. But it was also the beginning of everything that came after and my new life.

Coming out of detox wasn't a smooth transition into a brand-new life. It was more like a slow crawl.

Recovery, for me, offered a daily decision. And in those early days, everything felt unfamiliar. The routines I used to lean on were gone, and I had to create new ones. The coping mechanisms I relied on (mainly alcohol) were stripped away.

I had to rebuild myself from the inside out. I had to find out who I was.

But the difference this time? I wasn't trying to do it alone.

I leaned on God more than I ever had in my life. My faith became my foundation. I talked to God constantly. I had to reconnect with the truth that my value didn't come from my performance, on the field or in life. It came from the fact that I was loved, created with purpose, and worth saving.

Physically, things got worse before they got better. I developed ascites, the abnormal build-up of fluid in my abdomen. My body started retaining fluid, dangerous levels of it, too. At one point, I had 30 pounds of fluid built up in my stomach, and it was accumulating that heavily every week.

I looked like I was pregnant.

Every week, I had to go in and get that fluid drained. They'd stick a long needle into my side, give me an IV, and pump out the fluid. The pain was intense. Every time I walked out of that hospital 30 pounds lighter, it felt relieving but also painful. It was a constant reminder of what alcohol had done to my body. It was the price I had to pay.

One day, not long before a scheduled drain, my wife and I were at Bed Bath & Beyond. Just shopping. I don't even remember what we were looking for, might've just been killing time. My stomach was full of fluid again, stretched tight and uncomfortable. I was just trying to get through the day and to my draining appointment that was scheduled for the following day.

Then a store employee walked up to me, totally calm, and said, "Sir, can you put that pillow back?"

I looked at her, confused. "What?"

She pointed at my stomach. "That pillow," she said. "Put it back."

I was stunned. And embarrassed. Without saying a word, I lifted my shirt right there in the aisle and said, "That's not a pillow. That's my stomach."

Her face changed immediately, shock, maybe shame, but the damage was done. I wasn't mad at her. Not really. I was just... sad. Sad that I'd gotten to a point where my own body had become unrecognizable. Sad that a stranger could mistake my illness for someone trying to steal a pillow.

That moment stuck with me, not because it hurt (though it did), but because it reminded me just how visible our hidden battles can become. You can only carry pain in silence for so long before it starts showing up on the outside.

Five surgeries followed. Each one left a scar and added another chapter to the story I never thought I'd be writing. But every scar is a reminder; I'm still here. Still fighting. Still choosing to live this life. And thankful to God for giving me another chance. I don't deserve any of His blessings, but He blesses me anyway. For that I am grateful.

Day by day, I continue to heal. Not just physically, but mentally. Emotionally. Spiritually. Sobriety has given me new life. A life of meaning. And a life of purpose.

Today, my life is not defined by sports, or success, or addiction. It's defined by purpose. My faith is stronger than it's ever been. I live each day with intention. I focus on the people who matter most in my life and being the best version of myself for them.

And after twenty-four years away from the classroom, I made another decision: I went back to school. I'm finishing my degree at Oregon State University. I'm a senior, studying psychology, and I'll be the first in my family to graduate from a four-year university. Pretty cool.

But the number one reason I went back to school? My daughter.

I want her to see, with her own eyes, that it's never too late in life to chase something meaningful. Never too late to grow, to start over, to become more. I want her to know that no matter where life takes you, you can always rewrite your story. I want my life to be living proof of that for her. I want to inspire her.

And beyond that, I'm after understanding. I want to understand why we do what we do. Why addiction takes hold. Why people suffer in silence. Why so many of us carry pain we don't know how to name.

My mission now is to help people find their turning point before they end up on the floor like I did. To meet them in the silence and say, "You're not alone." To let them know a life free from alcohol or substances is possible, and that healing is possible. That our past doesn't define us or get the final say. We can be who we choose to be. All it takes is making a decision.

That is exactly what I did. I made a decision to quit drinking alcohol. To stop nicotine use. To begin the work of becoming the man I was always meant to be. A man of integrity. A man of faith. A man of purpose.

Because of those decisions, today, my life is rooted in something real. Something lasting. And for the first time in my life, today, I know exactly who I am.

Now I see someone I know when I look in the mirror, because…

I don't do that anymore.

Chapter 2: It Won't Happen to Me

We tell ourselves we're the exception. That addiction only happens to other people, people who are reckless, broken, or weak. But the truth doesn't care about our BS—our belief system, that is. Addiction doesn't discriminate. I've seen its effects on twelve-year-olds watching their families fall apart. I've seen it sneak into the lives of working-class parents who thought one glass of wine at the end of the day was harmless, until it wasn't. I've sat across from people in their sixties, still trying to outrun habits they picked up decades ago.

Addiction doesn't care how old you are. It doesn't care if your life looks put together. It shows up wherever there is pain. So if you're hurting, this is for you.

Maybe you're trying to keep it all together at work, at home, at school, and something inside you is fraying. Maybe you're worried about someone close to you who's slipping, but you don't know how to stop the fall.

Or maybe you're already knee deep in it, just looking for a way out. If you're a parent, your kids are learning more from your behavior than your words. They're watching how you handle stress. How you process pain. How you cope with disappointment. What are you teaching them without even realizing it?

If you're a parent, friend, coach, teacher, or mentor, your words matter. You might be the only voice in someone's life saying, "You're worth more than this." Don't underestimate the power of your presence.

And if you've already walked through it, if you've battled addiction and come out the other side, then your story isn't just your past. It's someone else's survival guide. Don't keep it to yourself.

Here's the truth: It can happen to anyone.

I don't care where you are in life. Whether you're in middle school or midlife, in a classroom or a break room, this message is for you. I am glad that you are here. That you're reading this. That something inside you is still open to the truth. Because this isn't just about addiction. It's about the lie we believe when we say, that won't ever happen to me. I believed that lie, until it did happen to me.

Before I get into that, here's something worth knowing: studies show that teenagers and young adults are statistically more likely to underestimate risk and overestimate their ability to handle it. They often believe nothing bad will happen to them because consequences feel far away and the future feels abstract. It's part of how the brain develops during those years, when decision-making isn't fully mature yet.

That mindset can be dangerous, especially when it comes to addiction. In essence, many young people believe they're immune to consequences. That mindset, the belief that "It won't happen to me," is often where the trouble begins. It creates just enough distance from the danger to feel safe while quietly moving closer to it.

Let me tell you a true story that happened years ago when I was in high school.

Back in 1998, four guys I knew were hanging out one night. Just being teenagers. Not causing any trouble, per se. I don't even know exactly what they were doing out that night, but whatever it was, they didn't anticipate the night ending up the way that it did.

They were on a winding road, headed downhill, when the car veered off and down an embankment. One of the boys suffered major brain damage. He spent a significant amount of time in the hospital and needed multiple surgeries. He almost didn't make it and is extremely lucky to be alive.

The driver's family, very wealthy, got sued by the family of the injured boy. And they lost. Lost their business. Lost their home. Their reputation. Everything.

That one night changed four kids' lives forever. But it also changed several other peoples lives too. Parents, siblings, extended family members, friends, just to name a few.

Here's the thing: none of them saw it coming. They did not plan on their evening going down the way that it did, and that's how it works. No one thinks they're about to make the decision that will destroy everything.

It always feels like just one more drink, one more hit, one more pill, one more whatever won't be that big of a deal. That kind of stuff happens to other people, remember? But, the consequences do show up, sooner or later. And addiction doesn't knock on your door and announce itself. It just creeps in. Slowly. Quietly.

Behind the scenes while using, it's robbing you.

Let's talk about what addiction really costs. Have you ever thought of that?

The financial hit alone can be devastating. Take a look at what just one DUI can cost on average:

- Fines and court fees: $1,000–$2,500
- Lawyer fees: $2,000–$5,000
- Towing and impound fees: $150–$500
- Vehicle repairs (if there was an accident): $500–$10,000+
- Medical bills for physical injuries: Can easily exceed $10,000
- Increased car insurance premiums: Up to $10,000 over several years
- License reinstatement fees: $100–$300
- Mandatory DUI education programs: $500–$1,000

- Lost wages (due to court dates or jail time): Hundreds to thousands
- Jail time: Typically 48 hours to 6 months for a first-time offense
- Probation and monitoring costs: $600–$1,200 annually

That's easily $10,000–$30,000 or more, for a single mistake.

And that's just the money. It doesn't even begin to measure the relational damage, career setbacks, or the toll it takes on you mentally.

What if someone dies? If you're under the influence and take a life, the cost isn't just financial, it's much, much more. DUI manslaughter can carry a sentence of 10 to 20 years in prison, or even more, depending on the state.

You're no longer just dealing with fines or rehab. You're dealing with the fact that someone's mother, father, child, or friend is gone forever. That guilt doesn't go away. You live with it every day. The people who loved that person must live with the loss, too. That can be unbearably painful. And it's a weight that no amount of money can lift.

Relationally, addiction wrecks people. It destroys trust, and what is a relationship without trust? Not much of a relationship at all. Then, everything else starts to fall apart.

You stop being someone people can count on. You lie to cover your tracks. You make promises you don't keep. You show up late, or not at all. The people who love you start to feel like they don't know you anymore. At first, they make excuses for you.

They believe what you say. They try to help. But eventually, they get tired of the chaos. Tired of the lies. Tired of hoping you'll change.

So they pull back. Or you push them away before they can. You lose people. Not because they didn't care, but because they didn't know what else to do. All the while, deep down, you knew it didn't have to be that way.

Addiction makes you say things you regret. Do things you never thought you would. It turns love into pain and connection into distance. It makes home feel cold. It turns laughter into tension. It changes the way people look at you, and the way you look at yourself.

And even if they stay, it's not the same. They don't trust you like they used to. They wait for the other shoe to drop. They flinch when your phone goes off or you walk through the door late.

You don't just lose relationships. You lose the version of yourself who knew how to be honest, how to be present, how to love people well.

Financially, it is expensive. Not just the cost of the alcohol or the drugs themselves, but everything that follows. Missed work. Lost jobs. Legal fees. Medical bills. Therapy. Rehab. Not to mention the opportunities you never get because of the damage that's already been done.

It can derail an entire career before it even starts. Scholarships vanish. Internships fall through. Trust with employers is broken. You can't network from a jail cell. You can't show up to an interview with a hangover and expect to make a good impression. Addiction narrows your future with every poor decision it convinces you to make.

Physically, it breaks you down. You age faster. Your immune system weakens. You lose energy. You gain weight or waste away. Your sleep gets worse. Your skin changes. Your organs start to fail. It might not happen all at once, but with time, it does happen.

Hangovers get worse. Your tolerance increases. The buzz you used to get from one drink now takes three, four, five. And every time you push that boundary, your body pays the price.

Mentally, it hijacks your brain. Your moods swing. Your anxiety spikes. Depression creeps in. You feel disconnected, numb, and empty. The thing you're using to escape ends up being the thing chaining you down.

Your confidence disappears. You start doubting yourself. The shame grows louder than your common sense, and the worst part is that you convince yourself this is who you are now, as if there's no way back.

Spiritually, it separates you from yourself. From your values. From your peace. From God. You start living in a way you never imagined you would. You feel the distance between who you are and who you're meant to be.

And if you're sitting there thinking, "But I'm not an addict," I want you to ask yourself a few honest questions:

Am I using something to avoid what I'm feeling?

Am I hiding it from people I love?
Do I regret things I've done while under the influence?
Is it still fun, or just a habit now?
Could I stop if I really wanted to?

You want to know what else addiction takes? It takes your time. And you don't get that back. Hours, days, entire years can disappear in the fog of substance abuse. Moments you should've remembered. Conversations you should've been present for. Milestones you should've celebrated. They're gone, and for what? A few hours of escape? A night you won't even remember?

Addiction steals the future you were building. One missed opportunity at a time. One broken relationship at a time. It never announces itself. It just tip toes in, settles down and makes itself comfortable. Unnoticed. Until it owns you.

Sometimes the people who are struggling the most are the ones who look the most put together. The ones who smile in public and appear to have everything going for them, but they are miserable behind closed doors and cry when no one can see them. The ones who carry the weight of the world on their shoulders but don't let it show. Maybe that's you. Maybe you've mastered the art of hiding it. Maybe even your closest friends don't know how bad it's gotten.

The moment when you finally tell the truth. That's the beginning of healing.

I had to face a lot of hard truths in my own recovery. Like the fact that I hurt people. That I disappointed people. That I let down people who believed in me. I had to own that. It wasn't fun and it sure wasn't easy, but it was necessary in order for me to start my recovery journey and the healing process.

You might be reading this and thinking, "I don't know how to fix what I've broken."

Here's what I'll say: Start with today. You don't need to have the next year figured out. Just do the next right thing. Apologize. Ask for help. Show up. Be honest. Look to others who have gone through what you are going through. Get quiet and talk to God. Let Him guide the next step.

There's no perfect formula for recovery, and everyone's recovery journey is unique and different, but I can tell you what's worked for me and for a lot of people I know is routine, community, honesty, faith, and service. Build new habits. Stay around people who are walking in the same direction. Tell the truth even when it's hard. Pray when you feel weak.

You don't have to do this alone. There are people who want to help. Coaches, counselors, sponsors, pastors, teachers, mentors, just to name a few.

If the first one you talk to doesn't get it, don't stop. Keep reaching out until someone does. There are hotlines, support groups, churches, recovery centers. There are people who've been where you are, and they made it out. You can too.

It's not about willpower. It's about surrender. It's about choosing something greater than your addiction. Choosing faith. Choosing freedom. Choosing the future over the moment.

Choosing to no longer live the way you used to. Choosing to be the person you want to become.

I don't know what your rock bottom looks like. Maybe it's quiet. Maybe it was loud. Maybe you haven't hit it yet. Or maybe you've already been there and you're just trying to crawl out.

Wherever you are, you don't have to stay there. You don't have to wait for everything to collapse before you change. You don't need a disaster to justify getting help. You just need to decide you're done with the direction things are going.

This doesn't have to be the end of your story.

You don't have to wait for everything to fall apart before you change. You don't need to hit rock bottom to ask for help. You just need to be done. Done with hiding. Done with pretending. Done with pain that keeps piling up.

Maybe you feel stuck. Maybe you feel numb. Maybe you feel ashamed of what it's come to. But it's not too late. You are not too far gone. You are not beyond reach. The damage might be real, but so is the chance to rebuild.

You don't have to have it all figured out. You just have to move. One step. One choice. One conversation. Tell someone the truth. Let someone in. And know this: God is right there with you. Not watching from a distance. Not waiting for you to get your act together. He's in it. with you, beside you, right now. In the mess. In the confusion. In the pain.

So take the step. Make the call. Say what you've been afraid to say. Ask for help.

Do it unsure. Do it exhausted. Do it anyway.

Yes, it can happen to you. The spiral. The destruction. The regret.

But so can healing. So can peace. So can change.

You might feel like you've blown it. Like there's no way back.

But there is. And whether you believe it yet or not, you're still worth fighting for.

So how do you start?

You start by getting honest with yourself. Really honest. No more justifying. No more excuses. You ask yourself the hard questions. You admit what's not working. You stop pretending. And you invite someone in to walk this recovery road with you.

Find people who care enough to call you out. People who love you enough to tell you the truth. A mentor, a coach, a sponsor, a pastor, a friend, whoever. Build a circle of people who will hold you up when you're too tired to stand.

And above all, turn to God. Even when you feel far from Him. Even when you feel ashamed. He is not intimidated by your mess. He meets you in it. He doesn't wait until you're perfect to offer His love. He offers it now, just as you are. That's what changed everything for me. That's what keeps me going today.

I talk to God daily. Sometimes it's a full-on prayer. Sometimes it's a whisper. Sometimes it's just me saying, "Help me, Lord," or "Thank you, Lord." He is always there for me.

If you're still reading this, it means you haven't given up. So don't. Don't settle for surviving. Don't settle for numbing out or living halfway. You were made for more. You were made to live with purpose, with joy, with freedom.

It won't be easy. But it will be worth it.

Today, my life looks nothing like it used to. I'm almost three years sober. I'm back in school after more than two decades away. I'm finishing my degree in psychology, because I want to help people understand their pain and heal from it. I'm showing my daughter what it means to rise again. To keep going. To chase growth, even when it's hard.

I still face challenges. Life didn't magically get easy. But I face those challenges as a man who knows exactly who he is, who knows what matters, and who is committed to walking in truth. Not perfection, just truth.

If there's one takeaway from this chapter, let it be this: no one is immune. Addiction, loss, regret, those aren't just things that happen to other people. They can happen to you. The moment you think it can't is often the moment you're most at risk. And if you're not paying attention, it can all unravel faster than you think.

But healing can happen to you, too. Redemption. Freedom. A comeback. A second chance. A deeper purpose. All of that is possible. One decision at a time.

If I could say one thing to anyone feeling stuck, it's this:
You are not the worst thing you've done.

You are not your addiction, your past, or your pain.
You are a human being with value, with potential, and a future worth fighting for.

It might not feel like that right now. Darkness lies. But I've been there. I've lived through it. And if I can make it out, so can you.

Don't wait for perfect. Don't wait for permission. Start messy. Start scared. Just start. And then, keep going. One hour at a time. One decision at a time. One day at a time.

It worked for me. Your story isn't over. And the pen is in your hand.

What will you write next?

I used to think it couldn't happen to me.

I don't do that anymore.

Here's the truth: It can happen to anyone.

Chapter 3: Who Are You?

For a long time, I didn't have a good answer to that question. I didn't know, and the truth is, I had never really thought about it. As long as I stayed busy doing whatever I was doing, I could avoid asking myself the hard questions.

I thought identity was something you tied to what you did for a living or the role you played in life, not something you had to discover by finding out who you are.

When sports ended, I didn't just lose my daily routine. I lost the only version of myself I knew. My whole life had been built around being an athlete, the practices, the games, the workouts. It gave me structure. It gave me adrenaline. It gave me somewhere to belong.

When it was gone, I didn't know what to do with myself. The silence that followed was louder than I expected. I had no idea how to fill it. No more cheers. No more practices. No more sense of being part of something bigger than myself. I didn't realize how much of me was wrapped up in that world until it vanished, and it felt like I vanished too, in a way.

Without sports, I slipped into autopilot. I still got up. I still went to work. I still showed up in the roles I thought I was supposed to play: employee, partner, friend. On the outside, it probably looked like I was fine. Busy. Functional. Thriving, even.

But inside, I felt like a ghost, just moving through the motions, disconnected from all of it. I kept conversations light because going deeper was too dangerous. I stayed busy and told myself I was fine. That this was just what life looked like now. That feeling empty was part of growing up or moving on.

But the truth is, I wasn't fine. I was hiding. Hiding from the silence. Hiding from the disappointment. Hiding from the fear that maybe I had already peaked and didn't even know it. Hiding from the question I didn't want to face: Who are you, if you're not that anymore?

I didn't know. So I drank. I kept myself busy enough not to think too hard about anything. I told myself this is life now.

But underneath it all, the wreckage was piling up, both around me and inside me. The short fuse. Low energy. No joy. I was checked out, going through the motions of life.

Little things started slipping. My discipline, some of my relationships, my peace of mind. Nothing blew up. It just quietly unraveled.

The Wake-Up Call

It didn't happen in some big dramatic moment. I didn't know what to expect that day. Honestly, I was just there, not really all that worried. Still stuck in that "it won't happen to me" mindset. Just another appointment. Just another thing to check off the list.

But the doctor didn't waste any time. He looked right at me and said, "If you don't stop drinking, you will die." No pep talk. No soft landing. Just the truth.

And it hit me, not as some life-changing moment where everything made sense, but as fear. As clarity I couldn't ignore. Like the first crack in the wall I had built around myself.

Because the truth wasn't just about drinking. It was about the way I was living. It was about the way I had spent years pretending I was fine. It was about the mask I had worn for so long that I forgot who was underneath it.

That moment, in that plain, forgettable doctor's office, was a line in the sand. Keep numbing myself and die, or start actually living, even though I didn't know what that looked like.

I made the decision right then and there. I quit drinking.

But deciding to change and learning how to live differently are two different things. The real work, the honest, uncomfortable, day-by-day work, was just beginning. That conversation with the doctor didn't fix everything. It didn't heal all the damage I had done.

But it woke something up in me that I couldn't put back to sleep. It planted something in me that I couldn't ignore. A truth I couldn't drown out anymore. It forced me to face the one question I had spent years avoiding: Who am I?

Held Up by the People I Didn't Want to Let Down

When I look back on the turning points in my story, a few things cracked me open. One was a vision I couldn't shake. My daughter walking down the aisle someday, and me not there to see it because of the choices I had made. The other was a group of people who refused to let me fall through the cracks.

One of those people is a man named Alex Molden.

Yep, the former NFL player. First-round pick. Eight-year NFL career.

But that's not why I reached out to him. After I sold my company, I hired Alex to help me figure out what was next.

I remember him asking me one day, "Why did you want to hire me?" Without hesitation, I told him the truth: "God."

I had prayed about it. I wasn't looking for credentials in somebody, though he did have them. I was looking for someone who understood where I was at in my life. Someone who knew what it was like to lose the thing your whole identity was built on.

He did. He'd lived it too.

I thought I was looking for guidance, maybe even structure. But what I found was someone who helped me stop running.

We never really talked about business. That wasn't what I needed, and Alex seemed to know it before I did. From the start, our conversations pointed inward, toward values, identity, truth. Or as Alex likes to put it: "Alignment, Assignment, and Adjustment." And above all: character. Who are you when no one's looking?

It wasn't about building a plan. It was about rebuilding a person based on foundational principles.

Alex became more than a coach. We built a real friendship, but more than that, he became like a father to me. Not because he tried to direct me. He never once said, "Joey, you need to do this." He led with wisdom, strength, and grace. He showed me the kind of man I wanted to be. Not a copy of him, but my own man, shaped by character, integrity, faith, resiliency, and consistency.

He saw through all my BS. He didn't give me answers. He asked the right questions. The kind that made me stop, look inward, and be honest with myself for the first time in a long time. He helped me build a foundation I could stand on.

But Alex wasn't the only one.

My wife, my daughter, my mom, and my two closest friends— Sai and Bill—were right there too. They loved me before anything changed. Stood by me when I had no answers.

They didn't try to fix me or hand me solutions. They just showed up.

Showed up when I had nothing to offer. When I didn't know who I was.

They were there—through all of it. The good and the bad. And they didn't judge me.

I felt their support and knew I wasn't doing this alone. It gave me strength to keep going, and a sense of accountability. I didn't want to let them down.

And then there was that image, clear as day, of my daughter walking down the aisle someday, and me not there. Not because I didn't want to be, but because I had drunk myself into an early grave.

That picture is burned into my mind. It's the clearest reminder I have of what I stand to lose and the number one reason I know I will never take another drink again. Emily matters too much to me.

It wasn't just fear. It was grief. Grief for a future I was about to lose if I didn't wake up.

Between the thought of not being around for my daughter, Alex's honesty, and the steady presence of the people who loved me, something inside me changed.

It was the beginning of something different.

Beginning the Real Work

I knew I couldn't navigate it alone. I had tried doing it my way for long enough, and it almost cost me my life. I needed someone who could see through my excuses, my charm, my distractions.

I already had a coach at that point. I hired him to help me figure out what was next professionally, financially, and personally, which, at the time, made sense. I thought if I could just get the outside of my life straight, everything inside would fall into place.

But it didn't.

I stayed busy, but it was the wrong kind of busy. The kind of busy where you fill your days so you don't have to deal with what's really going on inside.

I didn't need a new plan. I didn't need another excuse to keep running. I needed someone who would slow me down long enough to face the parts of me I didn't want to deal with.

Someone who wouldn't be impressed by anything in my past. Someone who could see the cracks in the foundation. Someone who didn't flinch when I tried to hide behind jokes or charm. Someone who would call me out when I tried to lie to myself. Someone who helped me start asking questions. The right questions. The hard questions.

The truth is, I had gotten good at lying to myself.

Not in dramatic ways. In small, believable ways. The kind of lies that sound reasonable. The kind you can live with for a long time without realizing what it's costing you.

I told myself I was fine.

I told myself I was just tired.

I told myself everyone was stressed, and I wasn't any different.

I told myself other people had it worse, so I should just be grateful.

I told myself I could quit anytime I wanted and that I was still in control.

And every time I told myself those lies, I bought myself a little more time to avoid the truth.

It's easy to fool yourself when your life looks okay from the outside. When the money's coming in. When the job title sounds good. When people pat you on the back and tell you you're doing great. You start to believe it. You start to measure your life by what you've collected, not by who you're actually becoming.

At first, staying busy felt like progress. But deep down, I knew better. I wasn't building a better life. I was just buying time.

They didn't just ask about my habits. They asked the stuff that actually mattered.

- *What's your foundation really built on?*
- *What kind of man do you want to be, and what does it take to get there?*
- *Are you living in line with that, or just saying the right words?*
- *How will the book of your life read after you are gone?*

At first, I resisted. Hard. Because pretending is easier. It's easier to polish the surface than to deal with the foundation. It's easier to cut back on a few bad habits and call it growth.

Because working on the surface feels safer than digging into the parts of yourself you don't want to see.

And the scary thing is, surface changes actually work, for a while. You clean up your diet. You work out. You get some compliments. And for a minute, you think you're okay

But deep down, the real stuff is still sitting there, waiting. You can only avoid it for so long.

I had built a life that made it easy to stay distracted. Money. Opportunities. Attention. It all gave me just enough noise to drown out the parts of me that were breaking.

In the stillness, the truth gets loud, and deep down, I was terrified of what I would hear if I ever really got quiet. Sometimes I have moments where I still am, I suppose.

Surface changes don't heal soul wounds. And pretending doesn't heal what's broken inside you.

Eventually, I couldn't dodge the real work anymore. I couldn't outrun the deeper questions. I couldn't keep pretending I didn't know what was wrong.

If I wanted a different life, I had to become a different man, from the inside out.

And that started by getting brutally honest about what I actually valued.

Not what I said I valued.
Not what sounded good on paper.
Not what other people would clap for.
But what was real when nobody was looking.
What was left when all the noise died down.
What I would still stand on when everything else fell away.

Naming What Matters

I had to figure out what really mattered in my life.

When I got honest, it came down to four things:

Faith.
Health.
Family.
Purpose.

Simple words. But for me, they became the foundation on which the life I want to live is built.

So why did I choose these four things? I'll explain.

Faith, because my hope is anchored in the promises God made in His Word.

Promises that He is always with me, that He will never leave me, and that through Him, all things are possible.

Faith is what gave me the courage to believe that my life could change.

That I wasn't stuck.
That I wasn't too broken.

That I didn't have to stay the person I used to be.

Faith gave me the strength to step into recovery.
To get sober.
To rebuild my life on a new foundation.

It wasn't about trying harder.
It was about trusting deeper.

Faith is what keeps me moving forward when the old ways try to call me back.
It's what keeps me grounded when the storms hit.
It's what reminds me that even when I don't feel strong, I'm never walking through it alone.

Health, because I spent years taking my body for granted.

When I was an athlete, I pushed it hard without thinking twice.
Didn't matter if I was tired, hurt, burned out, I just kept going.
I expected it to bounce back no matter what I did to it.
I didn't think about what it needed, only what I needed from it.

Later, when the games ended and the structure was gone, I didn't shift into taking care of it. I just found new ways to tear it down.

Drinking too much.
Eating whatever.
Running myself into the ground without any real purpose.
Living like there were no consequences, like my body could take whatever beating I handed out.

I didn't respect it when I was training. And I didn't respect it when I was destroying it.

I used to think health was optional. Something you worried about later, when life settled down, when you got older, when you had more time.

But health doesn't wait for you to figure it out. It's that old saying: "Make time for your health, or your health will make time for you."

And it's true.

If I don't take care of my body, my mind, and my spirit, eventually I'll have no choice but to deal with the damage. And by then, the bill's a lot higher.

Health isn't about looking good.

It's not about some gym plan or diet or goal weight.
It's about honoring the life God gave me.
It's about having the strength to stay in the fight when quitting would be easier.
It's about having a mind clear enough to hear His voice when everything else gets loud.

Because when your health breaks down—physically, mentally, emotionally—you start shrinking.

You stop dreaming.
You stop reaching.
You stop hoping.
You stop living.

You just survive.

Recovery lives inside of this.

Because healing my health wasn't just about quitting drinking or chewing or running.
It was about rebuilding from the inside out.
It was about confronting the reasons I needed to numb myself in the first place.
It was about creating a life that didn't need an escape hatch anymore.

Health is how I stay connected to the man I'm becoming instead of the man I used to be.

Family, because when the dust settles and the crowd disappears, they're the ones still standing beside you.

Not the fans.
Not the followers.
Not the people who liked the version of you that was winning.

Family are the ones who show up when there's nothing impressive left to offer.

When you've messed up.
When you're not at your best.
When all the shine is gone.

They're the mirror that doesn't lie.
The ones who tell you the truth, even when it's not what you want to hear.

The ones who remind you who you are when shame tries to convince you you're something less.

Family taught me that love isn't earned by performing well enough or looking good enough.

It's given.
Freely.
Fully.
Even when you don't think you deserve it.

Family doesn't care how many medals you won or how many zeros are in your bank account.

They care about your soul.

They care about the version of you that doesn't show up on a scoreboard or a business card.

They remind me every day that life isn't about putting on a show. It's about being fully known and still fully loved.

Purpose. God didn't pull me out of the mess just so I could sit still. He rescued me so I could reach back and help somebody else.

Getting sober wasn't the finish line. It was the starting line.

Recovery gave me my life back. Purpose gave me a reason to do something with it.

If all I did was survive what I went through, it would still feel empty.

Purpose is what makes sure everything I fought through isn't wasted.

All the pain.
All the shame.
All the nights I wanted to quit.
It means something now.

But it's bigger than just doing good things. My purpose is to use my life, to use everything I've walked through, to glorify God and to help others.
To point back to Him, not to me.
To make sure the story being told isn't about how strong I was, but about how faithful He's been.

Purpose isn't about chasing titles or stacking up achievements.
It's not about building a platform.
It's about making sure the scars I carry don't end with me.
It's about going back into the places I used to be lost, and leading someone else out of that place.

My calling isn't just to stay sober.

It's not just to "be better."

It's to be proof that God still heals.
That comebacks are real.
That even when you think it's too late, it's not.

Recovery and purpose live side by side.

My healing wasn't just for me.

It was for the people still stuck.

It was for the people who feel invisible, forgotten, and hopeless.
It was for the conversations I haven't had yet.
It was for the lives I'm called to impact, not because I'm perfect, but because I've been there.

Purpose reminds me every day that freedom isn't about escaping pain.

It's about turning it into something powerful and purposeful.
It's about living in a way that every scar points to something bigger than me.
Something holy.
Something that can't be taken away.

Purpose isn't just about what I do.
It's about who I'm becoming, and who God is helping me reach along the way.

Living It Out

Naming my values gave me a foundation.

Living by them requires a whole new level of honesty and commitment.

It meant looking at the places where I was still performing instead of being real.
It meant asking myself hard questions when no one else was around to applaud or criticize.
It meant making decisions that lined up with who I said I wanted to be, even when it cost me approval, comfort, or control.

It meant walking away from relationships, habits, and environments that didn't support my healing.
It meant believing that wholeness was possible even when brokenness felt more familiar.

I learned a few things early on.

You can't just hope your life will change because you want it to.
You have to build it.
You have to see it lived out in front of you.
You have to find examples worth following, and follow them.

I knew I couldn't figure it out alone, so I started paying attention. I found people who lived the way I wanted to live. People who carried themselves with integrity, faith, and purpose. People who didn't just talk about their values, but actually lived them when nobody was watching.

I studied their habits. I watched how they made decisions. I noticed how they handled setbacks, how they treated their families, how they stayed grounded when life got loud.

At first, it felt awkward. It felt strange to admit that I didn't really know how to live differently yet. The truth was, I needed examples. I needed to see what it looked like to live with consistency and character.

Slowly, by watching, learning and practicing, I started becoming the kind of man I decided I wanted to be.

Change isn't just about stopping the wrong things. It's about starting the right things, again and again, until they become a part of who you are.

Turning the Mirror on You

I've told you how I lost myself. How I tried to stay busy instead of getting honest. How pain, not inspiration, finally cracked me open.

But this chapter isn't about me.

It's about you.

So take a breath and sit with it.

Ask yourself:

- Who are you, without the roles you play?
- Who are you, without the masks you wear to survive?
- Who are you when no one is watching?

Maybe you've been drifting.
Maybe you've been defining yourself by your work, your struggles, or your past mistakes.
Maybe you've been waiting for a wake-up call that hasn't come yet.

This can be that call.

The question isn't just "Who have you been?"
It's "Who are you becoming?"

You don't have to lose everything to find yourself.

You don't have to hit rock bottom to decide you're worthy of change.

You can start right now.

44

You are not your failures. You are not your worst moments. You are not beyond hope.

Your story isn't over.

You still get to decide who you're going to be.

The only question is: Will you be the one to write it?

I used to live without knowing myself.

I don't do that anymore.

Workbook: Getting to Know Yourself

(Take your time. Journal your thoughts. These aren't tests. They're keys.)

What's your wake-up call? Has it already happened, or are you still waiting for it? If you're waiting, what do you think it will look like?

What are the values that matter most to you right now? *(Circle or write your top 5, or add your own.)*

Where in your life are you living against your values?

What roles or habits are you using to avoid facing yourself?

If nothing changed, what would your life look like in 5 years?

If everything changed, who could you become?

Who are you without the mask of addiction?

What core values guide your daily decisions?

What would it take for you to make a permanent life change?

How do your choices affect your family, friends, and coworkers?

What kind of parent, partner, or friend do you want to be?

What kind of legacy do you want to leave?

Chapter 4: How You Can Succeed In Recovery

Let's start with this: there is no single blueprint for recovery. It is individualized, and no two recoveries are the exact same. Anyone who tells you otherwise is probably either selling something or has never been in recovery themselves. Recovery is a journey, imperfect, but forward. It doesn't offer step-by-step directions or instant clarity. But it leads somewhere worth going. It's not quick, and it's not easy, but it's one of the most meaningful things you'll ever choose to do.

"What would change if you got honest, really honest?"

Change Starts With Brutal Honesty

*The first step toward a successful recovery is
brutal honesty.*

Honesty with yourself. With others. With the patterns you've been justifying. You don't need to shame yourself; you've probably done plenty of that already. But you do need to get real. Because nothing changes until you do.

"When was the last time you didn't feel the need to perform or pretend, or to be someone you're not?"

More Than Sobriety: This Is Total Transformation

Recovery is about change.

It is not just quitting alcohol or whatever substance you've used to cope. That's just the starting line. The external behavior is only one piece of the puzzle. Real recovery reaches into every part of your life. Your habits, your relationships, your thoughts, your identity.

It's about becoming the kind of person who can face their life with presence and strength, who no longer has to numb, run, or disconnect just to make it through the day.

This isn't about surface-level improvements or slight behavioral upgrades. It's not about appearing more put together while keeping the same broken patterns underneath. Recovery demands a different kind of transformation. One that reaches into every part of who you are and how you live.

It's not quick. It's not easy. But it is deep, honest, and worth everything it takes.

This isn't about tweaks or minor adjustments. It's not about doing what you were doing, just a little cleaner or neater. This is transformation. Deep, uncomfortable, necessary transformation. The kind that touches every part of your life.

It's a full reset. A deep reworking of how you think, how you act, and how you show up in your own life.

You're not just quitting a habit. You're rewiring your brain. Recovery directly affects your brain's neurotransmitters, the chemical messengers responsible for mood, motivation, and impulse control.

When you stop using the substances or behaviors that flooded your system, your brain has to relearn balance. That takes time, consistency, and new forms of stimulation like movement, connection, and rest. It's not just psychological, it's biological. You're rebuilding the system from the inside out.

That kind of change requires more than just wanting it. It takes discomfort, discipline, and a steady willingness to keep showing up, especially when progress feels small, or nothing seems to be changing.

If your habits are shaping your future, what future are they building?

It might mean facing traumas you've buried for years. It might mean having awkward, painful conversations with family. It might mean forgiving others, and forgiving yourself. These aren't easy things to do, but they are necessary.

Recovery isn't just about removing something harmful. It's about building something better. Stronger routines, honest relationships, and a mindset that serves your healing instead of sabotaging it. It's about learning to love yourself more. To care for your recovery like you'd care for something sacred. Because it is. It's the foundation of everything else you want to rebuild.

Your Environment Matters. Choose It With Care

If you're serious about recovery, one of the first things you'll likely need to change is your environment. That often means your friend group. That's not easy, especially if you've been surrounded by people who enable your habits or who are tied to a version of you that you're trying to leave behind. But you can't build a new life while dragging your old one behind you.

Who supports the version of you you're becoming? Who pulls you back to the one you've outgrown?

You might love some of those people. That doesn't make them right for your recovery. What you need are people who love you, support you, and genuinely want to see you succeed.

Just as important, you need to love yourself and your recovery. You must protect both at any cost. You need to decide that your growth matters more than staying comfortable. It's choosing to honor the version of you that's trying to emerge, even when that choice means walking away from what's familiar.

You're rebuilding your life. That means protecting your peace, your energy, and your direction, without apology.

Changing your friends can feel like grief. It's a real loss. But it's also a step toward something better. Toward peace, clarity, and a life that reflects who you are becoming. It's a choice you make on purpose, because your recovery needs to be intentional.

Your habits are shaped by your environment, and if your environment doesn't change, neither will you.

The shift in your social life might be jarring. You might find yourself lonely at first. That's normal. Most people don't talk about that part of recovery, the hollow space that opens up when you walk away from the old life, but haven't yet stepped fully into the new one. It feels like floating. Like you've left something behind but haven't found your footing yet. That in-between place is where most people give up. Don't. That space means something new is being built.

Recovery Requires Connection

Recovery is not a solo mission. You need help. That might be the hardest truth to accept. You're used to figuring things out yourself, powering through, keeping up the appearance of being fine.

But recovery demands a different kind of strength. The strength to say, "I can't do this alone."

AA is a great place to start. For many, it becomes the first safe room they've walked into in a long time. I remember thinking it wasn't for me. I assumed it was for alcoholics, people with a label I hadn't yet accepted for myself. That was the first thing I had to admit.

But when I finally showed up, after being pushed by my counselor, I realized none of that mattered. In those rooms, I might not know the person sitting next to me, but I understand them, and they understand me.

We may not have lived the same story, but we've wrestled with the same struggle. Some people talk a lot. Some don't say anything at all. But either way, the common ground is there. There's a kind of mutual understanding you can feel without needing to explain everything. And for a lot of us, that's where things can begin to shift.

Walking into that first meeting felt uncomfortable. I didn't know what to expect, and part of me didn't want to be there. But looking back, it marked something important. It meant I was done lying to myself. It meant I was ready to stop hiding. It meant I was finally willing to do something different.

One of the common pieces of advice you'll hear is to do "90 meetings in 90 days." That might sound extreme, but there's a reason for it. The early days of recovery are fragile. You're building new habits, facing old demons, and learning how to live without the thing you've used to cope for so long.

Daily connection gives you structure. It gives you a mirror. On the hard days, and there will be hard days, it gives you a reason to keep going.

Not every meeting will move you. Some will feel awkward. Some might even feel pointless. But keep going. Eventually, someone will say something that connects. Maybe it hits you hard. Maybe it just stays with you. For some, it feels like a weight lifting. For others, it's just the steady realization that you're not alone.

If you can't always make it in person, most groups offer Zoom options now. You can show up with your camera off, just listening. You don't have to speak. Just be there. Absorb. Let the truth of other people's stories start to soften your own resistance.

Why AA Works for Many (But Isn't the Only Way)

Another cornerstone of AA is finding a sponsor. That word can feel weird at first. You might picture someone lecturing you or holding a clipboard. But a sponsor isn't a coach or a boss. They're a guide. Someone who's walked the path ahead of you. Someone who has been where you are and who won't be impressed by your charm, or distracted by your excuses.

Choosing a sponsor is about resonance, not résumé. Find someone whose recovery you respect. Someone who seems to live with the kind of honesty and peace you want for yourself. Then ask them to be your sponsor.

It's not a marriage. It's a relationship built on truth and accountability. If it doesn't fit, you can always choose someone else. But don't wait for the perfect person to show up. Just start somewhere.

You'll hear a lot about the 12 Steps in recovery spaces. Each step is part of a deeper process. This book isn't affiliated with AA in any way, shape, or form, and those steps are AA's intellectual property, so we won't list them here. What matters is that the steps are a framework for learning how to live differently. They're about change. They're about owning your life, cleaning up the mess you've made, and figuring out how to live with honesty, integrity, and clarity.

AA isn't the only path. Some people find what they need through recovery centers like Hazelden, or through therapy, coaching, or other support systems. That's not wrong. This isn't about choosing the "best" method, it's about choosing what works for you. What matters most is that it helps you get honest and stay connected.

"I thought strong meant silent. Turns out, the moment I asked for help was the first time I actually showed strength." —Kyle, former D-1 athlete, current AA member

The Power of Routines and Daily Anchors

Recovery is also about reconnecting with the parts of life you had tuned out or pushed away. It's about learning how to be present again, how to feel moments instead of rushing past them. That might mean rediscovering things you used to care about or trying things you never gave yourself permission to enjoy.

Joy in recovery isn't always loud. Sometimes it's just feeling calm in your own skin for the first time in a long while.

One of the best ways to cultivate that joy is by building new routines and habits that support your peace rather than distract you from your pain. That might look like waking up at the same time every day, starting with a few deep breaths or a gratitude practice instead of grabbing your phone. It might mean ending your day with a simple question like, "What did I learn today?" or "What am I proud of?"

Gratitude has been part of my recovery from the very beginning. In those early days, I didn't take anything for granted. I was thankful just to wake up. Thankful to be breathing. Thankful to have one more shot at getting it right.

That mindset helped me stay grounded when everything else felt unstable. It changes your focus. It pulls your attention away from what's missing and helps you see what's still good. Building gratitude into your daily rhythm helps train your mind to look for progress instead of problems.

Journaling to Stay Grounded

Journaling is a powerful tool in recovery. It has nothing to do with being a great writer, it's about being an honest one. Writing gives your inner voice somewhere to go. It helps you track your patterns, notice progress, and catch the lies before they take root. Some days, you'll fill pages. Some days, it might just be a sentence. That's okay. The point is to create space for the truth to land.

Here are a few prompts to get started:

- What am I feeling right now, and why?
- What do I need today that I'm not giving myself?
- What lie do I need to stop telling myself?
- What is one thing I can do today to take care of my future self?
- What am I thankful for today?
- What do I need to let go of?
- Where did I show up with honesty today—and where did I hold back?

- What's one small thing that brought me peace, clarity, or connection?
- What is something I've taken for granted lately?
- Who or what brought me joy this week?
- What part of my recovery am I most grateful for right now?

The Power of Routines and Daily Anchors

Routines matter in recovery. Not because they fix everything, but because they give your day structure and direction. They help you stay grounded when your emotions pull you off course. These daily habits, no matter how small, are part of how you steady yourself. Part of how you keep choosing the new version of you, over and over again.

In the early stages of my recovery, one of the most important things I built was a morning routine that gave my day direction and a steady place to begin. I started waking at 4:30 a.m. The house was still and quiet. I'd sit with some guided meditation and a few pages of recovery reading.

Amos Lee would be playing softly in the background. His voice somehow grounding and uplifting at the same time. I'd cook myself steak and eggs, and cut up some fresh fruit. I'm not a cook, not even close, but that ritual felt nourishing, like I was taking care of someone who mattered. Then I'd watch the sun rise and take an early morning stroll around the neighborhood school track with my wife and our two dogs.

It was more than a routine. It was time with her, and it was time with me. Quiet moments that helped me reconnect with the man I was becoming. A space to slow down, reflect, and thank God for another day.

It reminded me how deeply God has blessed me. I didn't earn it, and I still don't deserve it, but He continues to love me, protect me, and guide me. I believe He's kept me here for a reason, and that reason is to help others find freedom in recovery.

Now, you don't need to copy my morning routine, though you can if you'd like. You just need to build something that speaks to you personally. Something that anchors your day in intention and peace.

Those quiet, intentional moments make a difference. They're where trust starts to return. Where you catch your breath and realize you're no longer living on autopilot and that you are starting to live intentionally.

No matter how you approach it, whether it's AA, therapy, a recovery center, or another kind of support, recovery takes consistency. Recovery is built on showing up. Sometimes it just means doing the next right thing. You don't have to promise forever. Just focus on today. One day. One choice.

You wake up tomorrow and face the same question: drink or don't, use or don't use? That's how you stack days. That's how it adds up. Some days, success is not picking up a drink. Sometimes it's just doing the next right thing. Calling someone instead of shutting down. Going for a walk instead of spiraling. Showing up for what you said you'd do. It doesn't need to be perfect. It just needs to keep you moving forward.

If You Fall, Get Back Up

Now, you might stumble, even relapse. Many people do. You might fall into old patterns. That doesn't mean you failed. It means you're human. Recovery isn't about perfection. It's about coming back. Back to truth. Back to the commitments you made. The quicker you return, the stronger you get.

Shame will try to tell you that you've lost all your progress. Don't believe it. You are not defined by your past. You create your future, one decision at a time.

Every day, you get to decide how you want to write the next page in the story of your life. Every day you choose honesty, you're building something real. Every time you choose connection over isolation, you're laying another brick in the life you actually want.

Let's pause here and ask some hard questions.

Take time with these. Write them down if it helps. Talk them through with someone you trust, maybe a sponsor, a therapist, or just someone who understands what you're working through. Let them guide you into the parts of yourself that are easy to avoid. These aren't just reflection questions. They're ways to get honest. To stop avoiding the parts of yourself that need attention.

- When discomfort shows up, how do you usually respond?
- Who in your life supports the version of you you're becoming, and who pulls you back to the one you've outgrown?

- Are your daily habits building the future you want or just numbing the present moment?
- When you feel the urge to give up, who do you call? What do you reach for?
- What does success look like for you today—not forever, just today?

These questions aren't easy. But they matter. Surface-level changes won't carry you through the hard days. But the truth will.

The Small Wins Add Up

Recovery isn't always dramatic. It's often quiet. Unseen. It's choosing water instead of whiskey. It's going to a meeting instead of a bar. It's saying "no" to the text that leads to somewhere you know may set you back in your recovery. It's deleting a number. It's setting boundaries. It's leaving the party early, if you even go at all. It's doing the thing you said you'd do when it's the last thing you feel like doing.

Eventually, the changes stack up. You start to feel different, not all at once, but little by little as time marches on. You start to feel proud of yourself in small ways. You trust yourself more. You don't need as much noise to feel okay. The pull toward destruction weakens. When it comes back, and it will, you're stronger than you used to be and ready to stare it in the face with the strength to overcome it.

Define Success One Day at a Time

Recovery isn't a destination. It's a direction. It's not a phase you complete or a chapter you close. It's a lifelong journey. A daily decision. A constant realignment toward truth, growth, and healing. It is a way of living.

There will be plateaus. Days where you feel stuck. Seasons where progress seems invisible. That's normal. Recovery is not always about momentum. It *is* about commitment, though. You might not feel like you're growing every day. But as long as you're walking in the right direction, you are.

It's not just about staying sober. It's about staying present. Staying honest. Staying willing to change. It's choosing growth even when it's inconvenient. It's showing up for your own life and the constant quest to be better than you were yesterday.

You may discover parts of yourself that you didn't know were there, strength you didn't think you had, compassion you never extended to yourself before, dreams you buried long ago. Recovery isn't just about fixing what's broken. It's about discovering what's possible.

You'll build routines that support your peace. You'll learn how to check in with yourself and regulate emotions without numbing. You'll redefine success, not as perfection, but as progress. You'll start to believe, little by little, that you are worth it.

You may find yourself drawn to spiritual practices, mindfulness, journaling, and service to others. You may discover that helping someone else through their struggle helps keep you grounded in your own. That's the beauty of this journey: it's not just about you, but about the kind of presence you bring to the world around you.

Recovery is an everlasting quest to become the best version of you. That version of you isn't built overnight. It's shaped by daily decisions and honest conversations. Choosing connection when you'd rather shut down. Getting out of bed when you don't want to face the day. That's how the new you gets built. Quietly. Consistently. One choice at a time.

Eventually, you start to become someone you respect. Someone who lives by values instead of vices. Someone who doesn't flinch when looking in the mirror. Maybe for the first time in a long time, you'll feel free.

That freedom doesn't come from perfection. It comes from showing up and putting in the work, especially when it gets hard. It comes from the courage to face the truth, to sit with discomfort, and to keep walking anyway. This is your work. This is your path. But you don't have to walk it alone.

A new life isn't given. It's built. Slowly. Daily. Intentionally.

A successful recovery isn't about becoming someone else. It's about stripping away the habits, the fear, and the patterns that kept you stuck, and getting back to who you were meant to be. You don't have to fix everything overnight, but you do have to be honest about where you're at, where you want to go, and what needs to change to get you there.

You've made choices you regret. You've ran from feelings and emotions. You've shut down. You've tried to disappear. But you're still here. Learning how to face life instead of fleeing it. Learning how to stay when things get uncomfortable.

And when the old patterns want to show up, you'll be prepared. You'll pause. You'll remember how far you've come. And you'll say it to yourself, for yourself:

"I don't do that anymore."

Chapter 5: Replacing Addictive Behaviors

It Didn't Start with a Craving
It Started with Sugar.

I was in outpatient treatment. Sober, but still raw. Withdrawals were behind me, but I was far from steady. Everything felt off. My emotions were all over the place, and my body was still craving the sugar it had relied on to replace the alcohol. The drinking had stopped, but the impulses hadn't. I started chasing the same feeling in different ways.

It didn't start with a plan. One day I just grabbed a bag of gummy bears. Then it was Skittles. Nothing wild, but enough to notice. I'd never really craved that kind of stuff before.

Same with the Red Bulls. Six to eight a day, no problem. They tasted good, sure, but it was more than that. I just wanted something. A little jolt? A little escape? Not sure exactly.

One day my counselor, Grant, noticed. I was pounding Red Bulls and tearing through candy without even thinking twice about it. He just nodded and said, "We'll deal with that later." He wasn't worried. He'd seen it before. My body was still chasing the sugar it used to get from whiskey. To him, it was simple: I was trading one for another.

Early recovery is messy. You don't go from chaos to peace in a straight line. You grab onto whatever helps you get through. Not because it's good, but because it's not killing you.

Sobriety doesn't erase the craving. It just means you're starting to aim it somewhere else.

The Root Isn't the Addiction

Here's something most people don't understand unless they've lived it:

> *Addiction isn't really about the substance. It's not about the drink, or the needle, or the sugar, or the chaos. It's not even about the behavior.*
>
> *It's about the pain.*

It's about the emptiness inside you that you don't know how to live with. The fear you've buried so deep you forget it's there. The wound you never stopped bleeding from. The lie you started believing about yourself a long time ago, and just kept reinforcing until it felt like truth.

Addiction starts there. If you don't deal with that, if you don't face the deeper part, it just keeps coming back. It'll wear different clothes, but it'll be the same monster. One day it's alcohol. The next day it's rage. Then it's porn. Then it's control.

Then it's needing to be seen. Or needing to disappear. The shape changes. The root doesn't.

For me, I swapped whiskey for candy. Then candy for cars. Apparently. All in search of that dopamine hit.

In the first couple years of sobriety, I bought eight different brand-new cars. That's not an exaggeration. Eight.

The first was a brand-new Mercedes S550. $150,000. I didn't need it. I barely drove it. I just bought it. I don't even know what I was chasing. Maybe a feeling, maybe just distraction. For a minute, it gave me something.

Then it didn't. The high wore off. I was bored again. Empty. So I sold it. Took the loss. Didn't care.

I bought the Mercedes. Then another car. And another. I wasn't building a collection or trying to show off. It just sort of happened. Buy something new, feel something different. At least for a minute.

Then I got the King Ranch. I'm a truck guy. Always have been. And I've always loved Jeeps. They are beat-up, rough around the edges, nothing flashy. Like me, I suppose.

I still have both. Not because I'm chasing anything. Just because they fit.

It was never about the cars. It was about trying to feel something.

No more Mercedes. No more Range Rover. Those were fun, yeah. But they were for a different version of me. A version who still needed things to look a certain way to feel okay inside.

It was really about the feeling underneath. The need. The high. The hit of control or identity or distraction. I wasn't buying cars, I was managing pain. Trying to outrun the stillness. Trying to fill space with motion.

Once I saw that, I started seeing everything else more clearly, too. It wasn't just the cars. It was all of it. Sugar, caffeine, nicotine, constant busyness, always being on the move. None of it looked that serious in the moment. Most of it felt like nothing. But when I zoomed out, I saw the pattern.

Addiction doesn't always look like destruction. Sometimes it looks like success. Like ambition. Like you've got it all figured out. But underneath, it's the same engine. Always running. Always chasing. Always trying to outrun the quiet.

Eventually, you either slow down and face it, or you keep feeding it until it burns you out again.

That stretch of time, those cars, those habits, none of it was about luxury. It was about learning how to be okay in my own skin. To stop trying to escape the quiet and actually live inside it.

When I finally got still, I saw how much I'd been leaning on, without even knowing it. Not just the cars or sugar, but the constant need to stay busy, to fix something, to chase the next thing. All of it was noise. Distractions dressed up as direction. None of it gave me what I was actually looking for.

All of them were just placeholders. None of them were permanent.

Finding a Healthier High

Here's something I didn't see coming: you can keep the rush, you just have to change what fuels it.

For most of my life, adrenaline came from chaos. From pouring a drink, chasing something new, trading cars, staying busy. From always chasing something. Always needing the next high. Always moving.

I called it drive. I told myself it was ambition. Hustle. But really, it was anxiety. It was addiction. It was fear, disguised as energy.

Chaos gave me something to manage so I didn't have to manage myself.

But it doesn't have to come from destruction. That same charge can come from purpose. From connection. From peace. From showing up and being present for your actual life.

Real fulfillment has a rhythm too. It's not about intensity, it's about depth. About being fully in something that matters. Not checked out, not chasing, just here. Present. Invested. And that comes with a charge that feels different and stronger. Cleaner. Like you're actually building something instead of burning it down.

Now the high comes from different things. From doing what you said you would. From showing up fully. From being proud of how you handled something hard. It might not spike your system the way the old highs did, but it means something.

You start to feel it when you slow down enough to notice what's real. When you stop trying to blow past every emotion and start learning how to live inside them. It's not a perfect process. It's slow. Awkward. Quiet. But it starts adding up. And what you're building is a foundation.

If you're doing this work now, it may not feel like much yet. You might still crave the intensity. The noise. The hit.

But little by little, new things start to land. You finish a hard day and feel proud instead of hungover. You show up to something that matters and actually remember it. You get through a stress spike without reaching for the old answer. That win stays with you.

The healthy high doesn't come screaming in. It sneaks up in those quiet moments when you realize you're becoming the person you used to hope you'd be.

Maybe it's a real conversation that doesn't turn into a fight. Maybe it's taking care of your body in a way that feels like self-respect instead of punishment. Maybe it's holding your boundary. Saying no. Staying present. Not needing to explain yourself to anyone.

Some days, it's something small. A sunrise you actually notice. A song you forgot you loved. A text from someone who says, "That helped." A breath that goes all the way down.

Other times, it's in the harder stuff. The heavy conversation you don't avoid. The moment you take responsibility and don't run. The feeling of choosing peace instead of chaos, on purpose.

The world doesn't always applaud that kind of growth. But you'll know. You'll feel it.

This isn't about chasing a buzz. It's about reclaiming your life. One clear, honest, grounded moment at a time.

I used to live for anything that could take the edge off. Now I live for what makes me stronger.

I used to survive on escape. Now I'm learning how to stay and fight.

It's not always easy. It's not always pretty. But it's honest and real. It leads to my growth. And it's how I choose to live my life today.

The Bigger the Goal, the Less You Need the Fix

At one point, my health coach asked me: "You want to be an addiction coach, so let me ask you, how's that going to feel when you're still addicted to nicotine?"

It was a moment of clarity. She wasn't wrong, she was dead right. I hadn't even thought about it that way.

I was free from alcohol, yeah. But I was still chewing. Still leaning on something. Still needing a way to take the edge off.

It was just clear. No defense. No denial. I knew she was right.

I told her, "Honestly? I'd feel like a fraud."

That was the first time I said it out loud, and actually meant it.

I couldn't tell someone, "You can beat this," if I was still using something myself.

Even if it was legal. Even if it seemed like a step up from drinking.

It didn't align with who I wanted to be, so I made the decision in that moment: I don't do that anymore.

Not because I suddenly hated chewing.
Not because I wanted to be perfect.
I quit because my vision meant more to me than my craving.

But there was something else that helped me get there. Something my health coach taught me.

She told me that if I wanted to quit for good, I had to reframe the way I thought about alcohol and tobacco. I had to mentally go from liking them to seeing them as ugly and disgusting. Not just bad for me, but repulsive.

I couldn't keep treating them like something I was giving up. I had to start seeing them for what they really were: things that took from me. Things that lied to me. Things that kept me from showing up as the person I'm actually proud to be.

So that's what I did, and the cravings started to lose their grip almost immediately.

I didn't want to be clean *ish*. I didn't want to be *almost* free. I didn't want to keep editing the truth when I talked to people still stuck in it.

I wanted to look someone in the eye and say, "You can beat this," and mean it.

This wasn't about forcing myself to quit. It was about realizing I couldn't keep living out of alignment with who I said I wanted to be.

Who are you becoming?

That question matters more than most people realize. It's not just about what you stop doing, it's about what kind of person you want to be? What kind of example do you want to set? What story do you want your life to tell?

Nicotine didn't make sense anymore. Not because it stopped working. But because it no longer fit the version of me I was becoming. It wasn't aligned with the life I was trying to build.

When your goal is clear, when your purpose has weight, the old fixes start to fall away. They don't own you like they used to. They start to feel small.

That's when real change happens. Not when you hate the thing you're doing, but when you love who you're becoming more.

I didn't let go of nicotine because I had to. I let go because my future matters more than my fix.

From Regret to Recovery
Regret Doesn't Disqualify You

This part's not easy to talk about for me.

I was there. At every game, every performance, every milestone, I showed up. But I wasn't always present.

Physically, I was in the seat. But mentally I was somewhere else, far too many times to count. I was always thinking about the next drink. Wondering how soon I could get back to it. Doing just enough to lie to myself about fulfilling my role as a father.

And I regret that. Deeply.

It wasn't that I didn't love my daughter. Anyone who knows me knows how much she means to me. But addiction dulls everything. You move through life in a fog. You stop feeling the good stuff. Even when you're there, you're not really there.

I can't go back and redo those years. But I can be honest about them. And I can make sure I don't miss the ones in front of me.

I don't carry regret to punish myself. I carry it to stay grounded. To keep perspective. To make sure I stay present now, fully.

Alex once told me, "Your pain is someone else's prescription."

That line is one of the reasons I'm so passionate about helping people overcome addiction. Because everything I went through, every mistake, every hard truth has a purpose now.

It's not just a past I survived. It's a story I get to use.

I lived it so I could lead someone else out of it.

Slowing Down to Live Better

Addiction taught me to speed up. Sobriety taught me to slow down.

I used to rush everywhere, mentally, emotionally, and physically. Always chasing. Always anxious. Always trying to stay one step ahead of the crash.

Now? I slow down. I breathe. I see things clearer.

I take in the moment and sit in silence when my soul needs it. I pray instead of panic. I respond instead of react.

I'm not perfect at this. I still slip into old patterns sometimes, overthinking, overdoing, trying to force control. But the difference is, I notice it now. I catch it quicker. I don't live there anymore.

Slowing down means I actually feel my life. I feel the joy, the fear, the hope, the heaviness. I used to numb all that. Now I live it.

Self-Discovery as the Real Coping Skill

Here's what nobody tells you: the most powerful coping tool isn't in a therapist's office or a meditation app. It's knowing exactly who you are.

That's what sobriety gave me. That's what recovery taught me.

I had to face questions I never wanted to ask:

Who am I when no one's watching?
What do I believe in?
What matters enough to suffer for?
What do I need to heal from?
What kind of legacy do I want to leave?
What will I no longer tolerate?

What kind of energy do I want to bring into rooms? What does freedom really look like for me?

These weren't quick answers. They took time. Still do. But asking them opened a door to real freedom. Real power. Real self.

Celebrating Without a Crutch

Good news came with a drink.

So did bad news.

That was the pattern for years. Celebrate? Drink. Stress out? Drink.

Didn't matter what the emotion was. Joy, anger, relief, fear, I handled it the same way.

So when I got sober, I had no idea what to do with those feelings. Especially the good ones. I'd get good news and feel... unsettled. Like I was supposed to mark it somehow, but didn't know how.

It took time to relearn that.

Now, I keep it simple. I might call someone close. Go out for a nice dinner. Take a quiet drive and breathe. Nothing big. Just enough to feel it.

Sometimes I write it down. Sometimes I pray.

Sometimes I just sit with it and that's enough.

I don't need a high to celebrate anymore. I just need to be present.

That's the difference now. Today it actually feels real.

You'll be in situations where people drink. Where someone offers you "just one." Where people don't get why you choose not to drink or use.

Let them not get it.

You don't answer to them, and you don't owe anyone an explanation.

Here's what I say when someone offers me a drink: "No, thank you. I don't drink."

That's it. Simple. Clear. No apology. No shame.

You don't owe anyone a story. You don't need their permission. This isn't weakness, it's strength. It's self-respect.

Sobriety isn't punishment. It's power. It's clarity. It's freedom. It's choosing to live in alignment with who you are and what matters to you.

Some people won't understand that, and that's okay. You're not here to make everyone comfortable. You're here to be honest with yourself.

At the end of the day, this isn't about convincing anyone else. It's about being true to yourself, and protecting what's important to you.

Ask Yourself These Questions

If you're in the middle of this process, early sobriety, deep recovery, or just thinking about it, ask yourself:

- What behavior am I using to avoid the hard stuff?
- What's the pain underneath it?
- What am I really craving?
- What would a healthier replacement look like?
- What's a goal big enough to keep me focused?
- Who am I doing this for—and is that enough?
- What story do I want my life to tell?
- What would it mean to live on purpose?

These questions won't fix it overnight, but they just might wake something up inside you.

The Line That Saved Me

There are moments, still, when the cravings hit. Not just for substances. But for the old ways. The old patterns. The old escape routes.

In those moments, I say the same thing, every time:

"I don't do that anymore."

It's not magic. It's a choice. One I make daily. One I own fully.

I've been there. I've lived in the numb. I've tasted the regret. I've seen what's on the other side of giving in.

And I've also seen what's on the other side of saying no.

It's peace. Power. Purpose.

It starts with a decision, and that decision is:

I don't do that anymore.

It's about refusing to settle for a life that's smaller than the one you were made for.

Chapter 6: Mental Toughness Beats Addiction

The Real Work

This is the part no one likes to talk about. The part that's not flashy or easy or instantly rewarding.

Changing your life is hard. Changing your mind is hard too. And the truth is, you probably won't change your life for good without changing your mind first.

You can try to quit the substance. You can stay away from the behavior for a while. But if you don't deal with what's going on between your ears, you'll either go right back to it or trade it for something else that does the same damage.

Over my time in sobriety, I've learned it's never really about the substance itself. It's about what we're trying to avoid, escape, or numb. Grief after losing someone. The pain of a breakup. The weight of old abuse or trauma. Coping with mental illness. Stress from work or school. Financial pressure. Family demands. Loneliness that feels crushing. Sometimes it's boredom, wanting to fit in, curiosity, rebellion, or trying to feel in control. Easing anxiety. Chasing instant gratification. Doing what's easy and available.

Whatever it is, it's something deeper that we're running from. Facing that honestly is part of the real work. You might need to talk to a licensed therapist or the individual who may be causing you these issues. However, most importantly, you need to identify and address the root cause rather than focus on the substance itself. That is the real problem.

We like to say we *love* our vice. That it's our reward. Our comfort. Our relief. But that's rarely the whole truth.

If you want to change, you have to stop accepting your own sales pitch. You have to ask the uncomfortable questions:

- *Do I really love all of it?*
- Do you love the rush—or the way it controls you?
- Do you love the relief—or the damage it does to your body?
- Do you love the escape—or the shame and regret that follow?

This is why you need discipline: the ability to see the whole truth, not just the part you like. The strength to choose what's good for you over what feels good in the moment. The honesty to stop lying to yourself about what its really costing you.

Real change demands the discipline to face all of it. To tell yourself the truth. To choose better, even when it's hard.

This isn't about willpower alone. It's about mental discipline. About refusing to lie to yourself. About doing the work most people can't or won't.

Addiction isn't just what you put in your body. It's the patterns in your mind. The beliefs that trap you. The lies you keep telling yourself so you don't have to change.

You have to change the way you think about what you used to reach for. You have to stop seeing it as comfort or reward or stress relief, and see it for what it really is: a lie that does nothing but steal from you.

You don't change your thinking once and for all. It's a daily commitment. You do it over and over, every day. It's hard work. It's repetition. It's teaching your brain new responses after years of choosing the easy way out.

You're not just cutting out a behavior. You're committing to the discipline of choosing what's right, even when it's the hardest option. It isn't something you decide once and forget. It's a choice you make over and over, every single day. It has to become a new daily way of living.

Change the Narrative

One of the hardest mental battles in this process is changing the story you tell yourself.

I had to stop romanticizing drinking. Quit acting proud that no one could outdrink me. Stop telling myself it was my reward at the end of the day. Stop pretending it was harmless or normal or made me look social.

The truth was, it was none of those things. For me, and for many others on the same road, it was destruction, a lie that promised relief and delivered regret. You have to see it for what it is. Stop telling yourself it wasn't that bad or that you "deserve it." You've got to be honest. It's not a reward. It's a lie you keep telling yourself.

Your brain is sneaky. It will try to negotiate. Minimize. Tell you you're fine now or in control. You have to shut that down. Don't think of it as something you're giving up. See it for what it is, something you don't want anymore. Be honest about it, even when it's hard.

Let's Talk About the Lies

This is the part a lot of people ignore. The part that's not fun to admit.

Your brain is good at lying to you. Especially when you're stressed, tired, angry, lonely, or bored. It knows exactly what to say to get you to justify going back.

You have to be able to see these lies for what they are. Here are some of the most common ones:

"Just one won't hurt."
That's the classic. It sounds reasonable, like you're in control. But it's just the door back to everything you're trying to leave behind.

"I can handle it now."
This one shows up when you've had some time away. When things feel calmer. You start believing you're not that person

82

anymore. But you didn't stop because you could handle it. You stopped because you couldn't.

"It wasn't that bad."

Your brain loves to rewrite history. It'll minimize the damage, forget the shame, focus on the good moments. That's not honesty—that's denial dressed up.

"I deserve it."

This one sounds like self-care. "I've had a hard day." But real self-care doesn't sabotage your life.

"Everyone else does it."

Comparison will kill you. Just because someone else can use normally doesn't mean you can. You know whether or not that's you.

This is why you need discipline: to catch these lies as they show up. To challenge them. To replace them with the truth, even when you don't want to.

Because if you don't, they'll drag you right back to where you started.

Neuroplasticity and Repetition

Your brain can change.

It's not easy. It's not quick. But it's possible.

Over time, your brain learned to link stress relief, celebration, boredom, anger—whatever it was—to using. Every time you reached for it, you strengthened that association. It became the default pathway, the automatic response.

Those connections don't disappear overnight just because you decide to quit. They're built from repetition. That's why they're strong. And that's why you have to put in the work to change them.

This is where neuroplasticity comes in. Neuroplasticity is the brain's ability to reorganize itself by forming new neural connections. It's not some catchy phrase; it's how learning happens at a physical level in your brain.

When you keep choosing the same response over and over, like reaching for the substance to cope, to celebrate, or to avoid, you literally reinforce and strengthen those neural pathways. They become well-worn routes your brain can travel without effort.

Change means interrupting that automatic path and practicing a new one. Every time you choose a healthier response, pausing instead of reacting, sitting with discomfort instead of numbing it, telling the truth instead of lying to yourself, you're laying down a new connection.

At first, that new path is weak, unfamiliar, and uncomfortable. Your brain will want to default back to what's easy and known. That's why it feels so hard.

With repetition, that new pathway grows stronger. Over time, it can become your new default. That's why daily choices matter so much. Change isn't about a single big decision that fixes everything forever. It's about hundreds of small decisions, made day after day, that gradually retrain your mind.

That's how change becomes real, but it doesn't happen automatically. It doesn't happen just because you want it to. It happens because you keep being intentional about it. Even when you don't feel like it, and even when you're tempted to give up and give in.

Changing your brain is possible, but it requires consistent, deliberate work.

Discipline Over Motivation

A lot of people wait until they *feel* like doing the right thing. They tell themselves they'll change when they're ready, when they're motivated, when it feels easier. But that's a mistake. Motivation is unreliable, especially on the hardest days. It's fickle. It vanishes when you're tired, stressed, angry, or afraid. It doesn't always show up when you need it.

That's where discipline comes in. Discipline is what carries you when motivation fails. It's the ability to choose what matters over what's easy. It's making the right choice even when it feels uncomfortable, boring, or painful.

Discipline is telling your cravings "no" when every part of you is screaming "yes."
Discipline is sticking to your plan even when it's inconvenient or annoying.
Discipline is going to bed early when you'd rather stay up late and spiral through anxious thoughts.
Discipline is calling your sponsor or counselor even when your pride says you don't need help.

Discipline is being honest with yourself when denial would be easier.

It's not exciting or glamorous. Nobody cheers you on for choosing water over a drink. Or for walking away instead of lashing out, or for staying home instead of going somewhere tempting. It doesn't earn applause or instant rewards.

But it's the foundation of real freedom. Every disciplined choice is an act of self-respect. Every time you choose the harder, healthier path, you prove to yourself that you're capable of change. You teach your brain a new way of responding, over and over, until it becomes more natural.

Discipline grows through practice. It's like a muscle: weak at first, shaky and unsteady, but stronger every time you use it. And the more you choose it, the more trust you build in yourself. That trust becomes a lifeline on the days you feel lost or overwhelmed.

Sitting with Discomfort

Another essential skill is learning to sit with discomfort.

For a long time, we trained ourselves to run from anything that hurt or felt wrong. Stress, anger, sadness, even joy that felt too big or overwhelming, we didn't stay with. We numbed. We distracted ourselves. We escaped. We grabbed whatever gave us relief, even if it cost us later.

Recovery means learning to do the opposite. It means staying present instead of running. It means being willing to sit with feelings you'd rather avoid. To let them exist without needing to shut them down or smooth them over.

Cravings will come. Urges will rise like a wave. But they don't last forever. They peak, then they break and recede. If you can stay on that wave, if you can ride it instead of fighting or surrendering, you give yourself a chance to choose differently.

It won't always feel manageable. Sometimes the discomfort is intense and overwhelming. You might sit with it and find that it doesn't ease right away. That's normal. It's part of the process. It means you're doing the work, and practicing how to hold steady without giving in, even when it feels nearly unbearable.

Discomfort isn't dangerous. It's just uncomfortable. Your brain will tell you that you can't handle it. That you need relief right now. Prove it wrong. Show yourself you can sit with hard things without letting them control you. That's where real freedom starts.

When you stop running from discomfort, you take its power away. You teach yourself that you don't need to obey the urge. You learn that you're stronger than you thought.

Tools for the Mental Battle

You can't rely on raw willpower for managing cravings and difficult thoughts. Muscling through every urge without a plan rarely works for long. Having practical strategies gives you real ways to respond instead of react.

Here are some approaches that can help:

- **Mantras or Short Reminders.** A clear phrase can interrupt the urge before it builds. Something simple and decisive like my go to, *"I don't do that anymore,"* cuts off mental bargaining and reinforces your commitment.
- **Prayer.** A way to stay grounded and connected, while helping you feel less alone. It encourages humility, invites gratitude, and reminds you that you don't have to carry everything by yourself.
- **Journaling.** Writing slows your thoughts so you can see them clearly and challenge what isn't true. It helps you track triggers, recognize patterns, and hold yourself accountable. Just write honestly and let it all go.
- **Accountability.** It's easy to lie to yourself or get in your own head. Talking with someone who knows the real you makes it harder to keep those rationalizations alive. Saying it out loud breaks the hold those thoughts can have.
- **Mindfulness.** Pausing long enough to notice what's happening without immediately reacting creates space for better choices. Breathing, grounding, returning to the present. These simple practices can break the automatic cycle. I would encourage studying up on the practice of mindfulness, if you are unfamiliar.
- **Professional Support.** Therapy, counseling, or Cognitive Behavioral Therapy (CBT) can help you spot patterns and mental habits you might not see on your own. CBT focuses on identifying unhelpful or distorted thoughts and learning how to challenge and change them. If you have access to these resources, use them.

- **Routine and Structure.** Consistent daily habits like reading, prayer, exercise, gratitude, and reflection, provide stability when everything feels unsteady. They keep you connected to who you want to be.

These tools aren't shortcuts or guarantees. They're practical ways to make better choices when things get hard. The more you use them, the more options you'll have when it matters.

What to Do When You Slip Mentally

Let's be honest. Slip-ups happen.

I'm not just talking about using again. I mean mental slips. Those moments when your old thinking sneaks back in. When you find yourself justifying what you know is wrong. Romanticizing the old ways. Starting to tell yourself the old lies.

This just means you're human.

The question is, if you do slip up, what do you do next?

Here's a few things that can help:

- **Notice it quickly.** Don't let old thoughts run unchecked for days. Catch them early. Ask yourself: What am I thinking right now? Is this true? Is it helpful?
- **Name it honestly.** Don't sugarcoat it. Don't say, "I'm just stressed." Say, "I'm trying to escape." Don't say, "I deserve this." Say, "I'm lying to myself." Call it what it is.

- **Interrupt the pattern.** Move your body. Step outside. Call someone. Pray. Breathe. Write it down. Do anything that breaks the loop and gets you out of your head.
- **Get honest with someone.** Don't carry it alone. Tell a friend, sponsor, counselor. "Hey, my mind went there today." Speaking it out loud strips it of its power.
- **Refuse to spiral.** You're going to have thoughts you don't like. That doesn't mean you're starting over from zero. It means you're practicing. Treat it like training or practice. Every rep makes you better and gets you closer to your goal.
- **Reconnect to your why.** Remind yourself what you're working toward. The life you want to build. The freedom you want to earn. The people you want to show up for.

Mental slips are part of learning. Each time you notice and correct them, you're literally training your brain to respond differently. That's the work.

How to Build Mental Toughness in Daily Life

Mental toughness isn't something you're born with. It's not a personality trait reserved for the lucky or the strong. It's something you build, slowly, deliberately, one choice at a time.

It's not about pretending you're never weak. It's about refusing to stay there.

Here's how you build mental toughness in your daily life:

- **Do hard things on purpose.** Choose the challenge instead of the easy out. Take the cold shower. Go for the run you don't want to do. Have the uncomfortable conversation. The more you face discomfort willingly, the less it scares you.

- **Set small goals and follow through.** Win your mornings. Make your bed. Show up when you say you will. These might seem trivial, but they build self-respect and trust in yourself.

- **Tell yourself the truth—even when it stings.** Lies and excuses weaken you. Honesty—even brutal honesty—is the fastest way to get stronger.

- **Delay gratification.** Practice saying no to easy yeses. Skip the impulse buy. Wait to eat the thing you're craving. Training your brain to wait makes you stronger everywhere else.

- **Check your self-talk.** Don't label yourself as weak, broken, hopeless. Speak truth over yourself. "I can do hard things." "This feeling will pass." "I'm not that person anymore." "I got this!"

- **Embrace discomfort instead of avoiding it.** Cravings, stress, boredom, they're not emergencies. Sit with them. Don't numb them. Each time you stay present, you prove to yourself you can handle it.

- **Stay consistent.** You don't need perfect days. You need days that stack on top of each other. Progress is built over time, not overnight.

- **Lean on others.** Real toughness isn't isolation. It's knowing when to ask for help. It's the courage to say, "I'm struggling today."

- **Celebrate progress.** Don't skip this. Notice when you choose the better thought, the better response, the better action. Acknowledge it. That's how you see that you're growing.

Mental toughness isn't about being unbreakable. It's about refusing to stay broken.

It's not about avoiding pain either, but rather knowing you can face it, survive it, and come out stronger on the other side.

It's not about pretending you're fine. It's about doing what needs to be done, no matter what.

If you want to change your life, you have to train your mind. You can do it.

One honest thought.
One hard choice.
One day at a time.

Final Encouragement

Change takes root in how you train your mind. It's the quiet process of paying attention to what's actually happening in your head, owning hard truths, and choosing to respond with intention. It means telling yourself the truth when denial would be easier. It means sitting with what hurts instead of reaching for the old escape. It's standing back up each time you fall, however many times that takes.

This is the steady, daily work of building the life you want, through small, consistent choices that accumulate over time and shape who you become. It calls for honesty, patience, and a willingness to keep choosing better, even when no one is watching. One thought. One choice. One day at a time.

You're capable of this. But it takes believing in yourself enough to do the hard work, to face what you'd rather avoid, and to keep doing it even when it's the last thing you feel like doing.

I know because I've done it.

I used to take the easy way out, hide from the thoughts I didn't want to face, and run from the hard work of facing myself.

I don't do that anymore.

"If you don't quit drinking, you will die." *He locked eyes with me as if to make sure I understood. And I did.*

Chapter 7: Your Recovery. Your Story.

A New Perspective

You've made mistakes. So have I. But that's not where the story ends. You get to decide what comes next. Change doesn't just happen; it's something you choose. Sometimes in quiet moments, sometimes in the middle of pain. You decide to grow, to show up differently, even when it's hard. Especially when it's hard.

Survival may bring you to the edge, but intention is what carries you forward. That choice, made in the struggle, is the beginning of something better.

When I quit drinking, I didn't have a plan. I just knew I couldn't keep going the way I was. My body had reached its limit. I ended up on the floor, curled up and trembling. I was completely overwhelmed, physically, emotionally, spiritually. I couldn't move. I couldn't think. The only thing I could do was exist in that state of collapse.

Eventually, I was taken to the emergency room. My system was crashing. I was sick, dehydrated, and emotionally wrecked. It was the lowest point in my life, but it was also a moment of truth.

There was no more hiding. No more talking my way out of it. No more pretending I had it under control. I was in the care of strangers, and for the first time in a long time, I wasn't in charge of anything, not even myself.

They admitted me into medical detox for a little over a week. The days blurred together. The physical withdrawal was hard enough, but the mental and emotional fog was even harder. All the things I had pushed down for years started to surface. The guilt. The fear. The shame. There was nowhere to run from it anymore.

During that week, my coach Alex came to visit me. I wasn't expecting it. I was still in rough shape, still unsteady, but he sat across from me and didn't try to fix anything. He just showed up and was there.

But before he left, he looked at me and said, "Remember this moment."

He wasn't telling me to remember the specific details. He wanted me to remember how it felt. The vulnerability, the powerlessness, how low I felt, the rawness of knowing I never wanted to go back to that place again.

That visit didn't magically make things better, but it gave me an anchor. A clear, honest place to return to when the old patterns tried to creep back in. I knew what it cost me to hit that bottom, and I never wanted to forget it. Not to dwell in it, but to carry the clarity it gave me.

Recovery didn't happen the next day. It didn't even start to feel real for a long time. But something had shifted. I had stopped running. I had stopped lying to myself. That was the beginning. Not of a perfect path, but of an honest one. A path where I could begin to rebuild, day by day, decision by decision.

The negative voices didn't disappear overnight. I still questioned myself. I still felt like I had done too much damage. But now, there was something stronger underneath it all. A quiet awareness that I had a choice. And that choice wasn't just about staying sober. It was about showing up for myself, for my family, for the people who hadn't given up on me, and for the life I still had the chance to create.

The Role of Hope

There's a lie that runs deep in addiction and recovery. It's the belief that hope is something for other people. People who haven't screwed up as badly, people who still have something to look forward to. We tell ourselves that hope is for the naive. That it's soft. Weak. Unrealistic.

I believed that for a long time. I didn't say it out loud, but I felt it every time I looked in the mirror. Hope felt like something I couldn't afford. Like it would set me up for disappointment. Like it belonged to a life I'd already lost the right to have.

But what I've come to learn, slowly, and with a lot of resistance, is that hope isn't weakness. It's not denial. It's not pretending everything is okay when it clearly isn't. Hope is one of the hardest things in the world to hold onto when you're in pain. But it's also one of the most necessary.

Hope is what got me to that first meeting. It's what helped me stay through the first 24 hours sober, when everything in me wanted to bolt. It's what kept me from shutting down when I started facing the people I had let down and realizing the damage I'd caused.

Hope didn't make those things easier.
It just gave me enough of a reason to try.

A reason to keep breathing through the panic. To let someone else speak before I interrupted. To come back the next day.

I didn't trust it at first. I thought it would make me soft. But I started to see that hope is actually what gives people their backbone. It's what makes you pick your head up and say, "I'm not finished." Even when you're still surrounded by the wreckage. Even when nothing on the outside has changed yet.

There were days in recovery that I didn't want to get out of bed. Days when it felt like I was pretending to be someone better than I really was. But hope didn't ask me to be better right away. It just asked me not to give up. It told me that things could shift. Maybe not all at once, but piece by piece, over time.

There were losses, but many of them were by choice. I let go of people who no longer fit where I was going. Not out of anger, but alignment.

I didn't need certain conversations or drawn-out explanations. Just a quiet decision to walk a different path. Hope reminded me that becoming someone new meant making room for the future, even when it required letting go of the past.

Over time, something started to shift. I didn't feel fixed or whole, but I stopped believing I was only the worst things I'd done. I saw that trust could be rebuilt. That honesty could last. That maybe I hadn't lost myself completely.

What was good in me wasn't gone. It just needed a way back. Hope didn't fix everything, but it gave me enough light to take the next step. And then the one after that.

You still have that light somewhere in you. You don't have to feel it fully to believe it's there. You just have to keep going.

You Are the Author

If your life were a book, would you hand it to someone else and say, "Here, you finish it for me"? I used to live like that. I didn't realize it at the time, but I had stopped making real choices. I was reacting, coasting, trying to survive.

It felt like my story had already been written, and I was just walking out the last few chapters. Addiction had the pen. So did shame, guilt, and fear. I wasn't writing my story the way I wanted my story to read.

Recovery taught me something different. It didn't happen all at once. There was no grand moment of revelation. I slowly began to understand that I still had a say. That I didn't have to keep following the same old outline. The past wasn't erased, but it also didn't have to be the template for everything that came next.

Every day, we make decisions. Some big, most small. But all of them matter.

Every time you show up when it would be easier to disappear, you shift the story.

Every time you choose stay in the fight over running and hiding, you write a different line.

These aren't just actions, they're edits. Revisions. Proof that you're actively involved in the direction your life is taking.

There was a point when I realized I wasn't just living out my own story, I was acting out the roles that had been handed to me. The addict. The screw-up. The one who disappoints.

That label became my script, and I played it well. Until I didn't. Something inside me finally asked, "What if I don't have to be this anymore?" "What does the man I want to be, look like?"

Those questions helped me see that I had a choice. Not over everything, though. There are circumstances in life we don't get to control. But we always get to decide what we do next. We get to decide whether to stay down or get back up. Whether to stay silent or speak truth. Whether to stay stuck or take one small step forward. Whether we do what feels good or what we know is the right thing.

This is the book that is the story of your life. What do you want it to say? What do you want it to read like when someone else picks it up, or when you look back on it yourself? You may not have chosen the beginning, but the ending is still unwritten. Every line from this point on is yours to shape.

The power to direct your own life isn't something that anyone else can give you. It's not found in advice or approval. It starts the moment you stop waiting for permission. The moment you stop asking who's going to fix everything and instead ask, "What can *I* do now?"

If you're still waiting for someone to save you, stop. No one's coming to do it for you. This work is yours. You know what it's cost you to get here. You know what needs to change. And you're the only one who can decide it's time.

Being your own hero doesn't mean being perfect. It means refusing to stay in the same chapter when you know it's time to move forward. It means writing a story you can live with. One that reflects who you're becoming, not just where you've been.

You are the author. The pages ahead are still blank. Whether it's a sentence, a paragraph, or just one solid word. You get to write the next line.

The Power of Small Choices
Recovery wasn't one big moment. It was a hundred small ones. Quiet choices, barely noticeable at the time, that slowly

started to stack. No breakthroughs, just steady steps in a better direction.

It was choosing not to get high when I had the chance. Choosing to show up for my responsibilities even when I felt like disappearing. Picking up a book instead of the bottle. Sitting with discomfort instead of trying to numb it. Being honest when lying would have been easier, and maybe even expected.

I never really had the urge to drink again. After hearing the truth from the doctor, something in me shifted. I knew what was at risk, and I didn't want to go back. It wasn't about white-knuckling through cravings. It was about learning how to live without the thing I used to reach for.

There were hard days, no question. Quiet moments where I had to sit with things I used to try to escape. But I didn't run. I picked up *Meditations* by Marcus Aurelius. Or the Bible. I read until I felt steady again. Then I got up and kept going.

No one singular choice will make everything better. But it can keep us on track for one more day. That's how recovery happens, not in leaps, but in steps. Small, intentional steps that move you forward even when everything in you wants to fall back.

We tend to think we need some massive moment to turn things around. But most of the time, it comes down to doing the next right thing. Not the perfect thing. Not the easiest thing. Just the right one.

I didn't rebuild my life with a single transformation. I rebuilt it by choosing differently, day after day. Some days were straightforward. Others felt impossible. But each time I chose recovery over relapse, growth over comfort, truth over avoidance, I laid another brick.

Eventually, those bricks became something steady. A path I could walk, day by day, choice by choice, into a life I want to live, on purpose.

The big changes get the attention, but it's the small, quiet choices that build the life you actually want.

Every now and again people will ask me: *"How do you stay sober?"* My answer is always the same, *"One day at a time."* I wake up every morning with the same choice in front of me: drink or no drink. I choose no today.

And when tomorrow comes, I'll choose again. That's how I've made it this far. Not by figuring it all out in advance, but by making the right choice for this day, this moment.

Small choices, made over and over again, become a way of life. That's what recovery is built on.

Resilience and Recovery

Resilience isn't about being perfect. It's not getting everything right or avoiding failure. It's about showing up, even when you've fallen. It's about standing back up, even when you're tired. It's about continuing the work, even when you don't feel strong.

I remember playing sports and having coaches who drilled that into us. After a hard sprint or a brutal drill, they wouldn't let us bend over with our hands on our knees. We had to stand up straight, hands behind our heads, and breathe. It wasn't about pretending we weren't exhausted; it was about learning how to stay composed under pressure. How to hold your posture even when your body wanted to give out.

That same principle applies in recovery. You don't collapse into the struggle. You face it. You breathe through it. You stay upright, even when everything in you wants to fold.

I've had bad days. Days when I felt like I couldn't do it anymore. I've disappointed people who believed in me. I've had to sit in rooms I didn't want to be in and own up to things I never thought I'd say out loud.

But every time I've fallen, I've gotten back up. Sometimes fast. Sometimes slow. But I got up.

Recovery isn't a clean, straight path. It's full of detours. Setbacks. Gut checks. You don't walk it in a straight line, you climb it, crawl through it, and sometimes barely inch forward. But forward is forward. Progress isn't always obvious. Sometimes it's just choosing not to give up today.

You don't have to pretend everything's okay. You don't have to act like you've got it all figured out. What matters is that you believe the next step counts more than the last misstep. That's where your strength lives. In the decision to keep moving.

You've already shown that strength. If you're reading this, you've survived something. Maybe a lot. Maybe more than most people will ever understand. Look at that. That's toughness. You didn't avoid the hard things. You've gone through them and you're still here.

Give yourself credit for the things no one saw. For the nights you stayed sober. For the times you told the truth when it would've been easier to lie. For the mornings you got up and went to work when it felt like the world was sitting on your chest. Every one of those moments matters. Every one of them adds up.

I used to think resilience meant nothing could break me. Now I know it's showing up even when you already feel broken. It's doing the work when you least feel like it.

We all fall. We all stumble. That's part of the deal. The difference is what you do after. Stumbling doesn't mean stopping. Let your falls teach you. Let your scars tell the truth. Not about how you failed, but about where you've been and how you came back.

One of the most powerful things I ever did was stop hiding my struggle. For a long time, I thought I had to pretend. To act like I was stronger than I felt. But that only kept me stuck. And the truth is, most people already knew I had a drinking problem. I wasn't hiding anything from anyone. The moment I started owning my story, things began to change for the better.

Resilience isn't about perfection. It's about persistence. It's about choosing, again and again, to stand tall when life tries to knock you down. Just like those early practices, it's about catching your breath, standing up straight, and getting ready to go again.

Final Message / Sendoff

This isn't the end of your story. This is a new chapter. One that you get to write. Not the people you've hurt. Not the mistakes you've made. Not the voice in your head that keeps trying to convince you you're stuck. You're not stuck, you're just starting.

You don't have to wait for everything to make sense. You don't need to have all the answers. You just need to make the next right choice. And then another. That's where it all begins.

Right now, you have the power to do something different. One decision. One sentence. One page at a time. You don't have to fix your whole life in a day. You just have to stop writing the same line over and over again. That starts with you.

Whatever you've done, whatever shame or regret you're still carrying, you don't have to keep dragging it forward. You can lay it down. You can breathe. You can decide what comes next. Not out of guilt, but out of purpose. Out of self-respect. Out of a desire for something real.

Your chapter, your book, your life, is not finished. Not even close. It's yours. And if you don't like what the last few pages say, start writing new ones. Take ownership and control over your life. Create your tomorrow.

People ask me how I stay clean. How I stay honest. How I keep going when the past still pulls at me like it owns a piece of me. The answer isn't complicated. I made a decision. And I keep making it, over and over, no matter how I feel, no matter what the day brings.

I used to live without intention.

I don't do that anymore.

If I wanted a different life, I had to become a different man, from the inside out.

Chapter 8: Faith, Hope, & God's Role in My Sobriety

Seeds of Faith

Before I ever understood what grace was, or how deeply I'd come to rely on it, my mom made sure we were in church. Lents Baptist Church, every Sunday, rain or shine, cold or hot, whether we wanted to go or not. I still remember those itchy Sunday-best clothes, squirming in the pews while the choir sang and the preacher spoke.

I see now that those Sunday mornings at Lents Baptist, those clothes, that music, those wooden pews, weren't just tradition. They were preparation. Seeds planted by a mother who wanted her kids raised in the presence of God. And when I came undone later in life, those seeds bloomed. I am forever grateful for my mother's choice.

I sang in Awana, too, our church's children's choir. I stood proudly with the other kids and shouted out, "I may never march in the infantry, ride in the cavalry, shoot the artillery...

but I'm in the Lord's army!" We sang it like we meant it. And even though my walk with the Lord drifted in my teenage years and early adulthood, those early seeds of faith never really left me. I see now that God used those childhood moments to anchor me, to draw me back when I was ready.

Later in life, after wandering far from God during college and into my adult years, I found myself slowly returning to church, but it wasn't on my own. It was my wife who pushed us, even when I resisted. She wanted us to raise our daughter with a foundation of faith, and she believed we needed that too. There were Sundays I walked into church and still had alcohol on my breath. I felt like a fraud. Like God didn't want me there.

But I went, and I kept going. Over time, I realized God wasn't pushing me away; He was drawing me back in. Eventually, that feeling of not belonging started to fade, even before I quit drinking. But my relationship with Him still wasn't what it should have been. That deeper connection came once I got sober, surrendered fully, and asked Him to take control of my life.

I knew I couldn't do it on my own. I needed His help.

The Illusion of Strength

I used to believe that if I was strong enough, smart enough, or disciplined enough, I could fix anything. I could power through. Muscle my way out. Clench my fists and grit my teeth and make life bend to my will. That mindset worked for a while, on the field, in business, even in some relationships. But addiction shattered all of that. It exposed the truth that strength, intelligence, and discipline weren't enough. It didn't respond to effort. It ignored my routines, my reading lists, my determination. It just kept pressing in, demanding more, until I had nothing left to give.

Where God Met Me

Addiction brought me to the end of myself.

> *When everything I had built fell apart and my strength ran out, I realized I had nowhere else to turn. And that's where God met me.*

Not after I cleaned up. Not once I had a plan. Not when I had proven I could stay sober for a certain number of days. I didn't have to clean myself up for God to meet me. He came right into the wreckage. Into the shame I tried to hide. Into the failures I couldn't fix.

He didn't wait for me to get it together. He stepped into the pit, reached for my hand, pulled me out, and carried the weight I couldn't bear on my own. And I'm so thankful. I wouldn't be here, in the early sobriety days or today, if it weren't for Him.

The Power of Honest Prayer

Psalm 34:18 says, "The Lord is close to the brokenhearted and saves those who are crushed in spirit." This verse tells exactly where I was. I was crushed. Maybe you feel the same way I did. In that place, though, God didn't shame me. He saved me. And He will save you too. All you have to do is ask Him.

At my lowest, I prayed the most honest prayer I've ever prayed: "God, I can't do this on my own. I need you." It wasn't poetic. It wasn't polished. It was real and honest, from a man with nowhere else to turn.

I believe that kind of prayer moves heaven. God hears the cry of the broken. He has mercy for the weary. He doesn't wait for polished words, He responds to humble hearts. It's not strength that moves Him, it's surrender. His empathy meets us right there in our weakness.

Daily Dependence

Sobriety, for me, has never just been about staying away from alcohol. It's been about learning how to walk with God in a way I never had before. It's been about unlearning self-reliance and relearning daily dependence on Him. It's been about trading control for trust.

It's also been about becoming the man I want to be, a man led by faith, grounded in purpose, and shaped by grace.

There are still days when the old thoughts creep in. Days when the enemy whispers negativity into my head and ears.

On those days, I don't pretend to be stronger than I am. I use the tools that I have acquired through my sobriety, and most importantly, I look up. Something about looking up to the sky always makes me feel so small in this giant world, and reminds me of who exactly is in control. My job is to just trust and believe in Him, and do the work I am supposed to be doing.

He will take care of everything else. He always has, and He still does. I am so grateful for that, too, to say the least.

John 15:5 says, "Apart from Me, you can do nothing." Jesus didn't say, "You can do a little." He said you can do *nothing*. That's the truth. When I stay connected to Him, I'm strong and can do anything. When I drift, I become weak and unravel. It's that simple.

His Strength, Not Mine

There's a verse in Isaiah 41:10 that I clung to in the early days of my recovery. It says, "So do not fear, for I am with you; do not be dismayed, for I am your God. I will strengthen you and help you; I will uphold you with my righteous right hand."

That verse wasn't just comforting, it was a promise. God wasn't saying, "Figure it out and I'll show up." He was saying, "I'm already here. Let Me carry you."

There were moments when I didn't know how I was going to get through the day. Not because I wanted to drink, but because I was finally facing everything I used to run from. The regret. The pain. The damage. The time I couldn't get back. Some mornings felt heavy with all of it.

I read scripture because I needed to hear something that gave me hope and was uplifting. Most mornings, that was it, just opening the Bible, reading a few lines, and reminding myself I wasn't doing this alone. That was enough to get my day started off in the right direction.

Grace Over Guilt

Recovery taught me that the goal isn't perfection, it's proximity. It's staying close to the One who can carry what I can't. It's being honest when I'm weak. It's letting God into the places I used to hide. In that daily surrender, I've found a strength I never had before.

Kobe Bryant once said, *"Until you've got to pick up that cross that you can't carry... and He picks it up for you and carries you and the cross, then you know!"* What a powerful statement that was when I heard it. Recovery taught me that kind of faith, the kind you don't just talk about, but live through. The kind where God doesn't just forgive your past, He carries you through what you can't carry on your own.

God didn't just remove my addiction. He began transforming my heart. He began healing the parts of me that used alcohol to cope. He began replacing shame with identity. Fear with faith, and numbness with purpose.

Sobriety wasn't my finish line. It was the starting point of a deeper relationship with Jesus. One that is built on honesty, grace, and daily surrender.

The Truth About Grace

One of the most dangerous lies I believed was that God was disappointed in me. That He was done with me. That I had messed up too much to be used again. But the more I pressed into His Word, the more I saw the opposite.

Romans 5:8 says, "But God demonstrates His own love for us in this: While we were still sinners, Christ died for us."

He didn't wait for me to clean up. He came for me while I was still in the pit. That's His love. That's His grace. That's the gospel. That is my Lord and Savior.

Today, when people ask me how I stay sober, I tell them the truth: it's not willpower. It's not self-discipline. It's not a twelve-step program, though I do have respect for those, and I know they've helped millions of people. For me, it's God. Every single day.

He's the One who meets me in the morning with mercy. He's the One who steadies me when I'm tempted. He's the One who reminds me that my past doesn't define me. He's the One who gives me the strength to do what I can't do on my own.

Even on the hardest days, He's still there. Still helping and blessing me. Not because I deserve it. Because of His love for me.

From Mud to Rock

Sobriety isn't some badge of honor I wear. I don't walk around proud of what I did, I walk around grateful for what God did. Every day I wake up sober is a reminder that He pulled me out of something I couldn't get out of on my own.

Psalm 40:2–3 says, "He lifted me out of the slimy pit, out of the mud and mire; He set my feet on a rock and gave me a firm place to stand. He put a new song in my mouth, a hymn of praise to our God."

That's what happened. I was in the pit. He lifted me out. And if I sing about anything now, it's Him, not me. Not my strength. Not my discipline. Not my story of "overcoming." Just His faithfulness, showing up when I didn't deserve it, staying when I wanted to run, and carrying me when I couldn't stand on my own.

Come Home

If you're reading this and you feel far from God, hear me: He's not far from you.

Acts 17:27 says, "God did this so that they would seek Him and perhaps reach out for Him and find Him, though He is not far from any one of us."

You don't have to get it all together. You don't have to clean up your life before you come to Him. Come as you are. Right now. In the mess. In the pain. In the questions.

He works there.

He met me in my rock bottom. He walked with me through recovery. And He continues to shape me every single day. Not because I deserve it or earned it, but because He loves me.

And He loves you too.

Whatever you're facing, whatever you've done, however far gone you feel, there is grace for you. There is hope for you. There is healing in Jesus.

Your story isn't over. Your failure isn't final. And you are not too far gone.

Come home to Him.

Isaiah 43:18–19 says, "Forget the former things; do not dwell on the past. See, I am doing a new thing!"

That's what He did in me. And that's what He can do in you.

Still Becoming

But let me be honest with you, it wasn't all immediate transformation. Just because I surrendered once didn't mean I never struggled again. There were days I still wanted to run. Days when shame whispered that maybe God had changed His mind. That maybe His grace had run out.

But every time I turned back to Him, He was still there. Patient. Faithful. Unmoving.

It reminded me of the story of the prodigal son in Luke 15. You know, the one where the son takes his inheritance, wastes it all, ends up feeding pigs, and then finally comes to his senses. What gets me every time is this: "But while he was still a long way off, his father saw him and was filled with compassion for him; he ran to his son, threw his arms around him and kissed him" (Luke 15:20).

God ran to me. Not after I got clean. Not after I proved myself. While I was still a long way off. That verse makes me tear up sometimes, because that was me. That was my story. Wandering far, wasting what I had, and thinking maybe I'd be rejected if I came back. But instead, I was embraced. Welcomed. Loved.

How I Fight Now

I still have to fight battles in my mind. I still have to silence the voice of the accuser who tries to drag me back into guilt and fear. But I've learned how to fight differently now. I don't fight in my own strength. I fight with the Word.

Ephesians 6 talks about the armor of God — truth, righteousness, faith, salvation, and the Word. I had to learn to suit up again, not like I did in my football days, but for something much bigger. Not once in a while. Every day. Recovery isn't passive. It's a war. A daily battle. And without God, I was losing. With Him, I continue to win.

What I'm Walking Toward

Let me share something else. I don't think recovery is just about what you're walking away from. It's about what you're walking toward.

For me, walking toward God meant rebuilding my habits around His presence. I started each morning in quiet time, praying, reading scripture, and talking with Him. I opened up to a few trusted people and let them speak into my life when I wanted to hide. I committed to church, not just as a place to go, but as a place to grow. God used those moments to reshape how I saw myself and my recovery. Galatians 6:2 says, "Carry each other's burdens, and in this way you will fulfill the law of Christ." I learned I didn't have to carry it all alone, and I wasn't supposed to.

So, if you're on this road and trying to do it all alone, don't. Find people who love Jesus and love you. Get around folks who will tell you the truth when it's hard and remind you who you are when you forget. We're not meant to walk this path by ourselves.

Freedom For Something

There is no shame in struggling. There is no shame in relapse. There is no shame in crying out for help. Romans 8:1 says, "Therefore, there is now no condemnation for those who are in Christ Jesus." Condemnation comes from the enemy. Conviction leads us back to God. If you fall, get back up. That's what grace is for.

And to the family members, the friends, the spouses who are loving someone through addiction: don't give up. Your prayers matter. Your presence matters. Your love matters. I had people who didn't give up on me, even when I wanted to give up on myself.

I think about my daughter. I think about walking her down the aisle one day, God willing. I think about the life I would've missed if I had stayed stuck. If I had kept running. And I thank God—literally every day—that He pulled me out. That He gave me another chance. That He never stopped calling me home and that He never turned His back on me.

I've learned to see my sobriety not just as freedom *from* something, but freedom *for* something. Freedom to love better. To serve better. To live with joy and peace and purpose. Freedom to be the man God created me to be.

Maybe you feel like it's too late for you. Let me crush that lie right now: if you're still breathing, God's not done. Philippians 1:6 says, "He who began a good work in you will carry it on to completion until the day of Christ Jesus." That means even when you're in the middle, God is still working. Even when you don't see progress, He's still faithful. Even when you stumble, He still calls you His.

I'll never pretend this road is easy. But I will say it's worth it. Every hard day. Every temptation resisted. Every prayer whispered in desperation. It's all worth it. Because life on the other side of addiction, with Jesus at the center, is wonderful. It's abundant life. It's what He promised.

John 10:10 says, "The thief comes only to steal and kill and destroy; I have come that they may have life, and have it to the full." I know what it's like to be stolen from. To feel dead inside. But now I know what it's like to live full. Not perfect, but full. Full of hope. Full of grace. Full of purpose.

And it's all because of Him.

So I'll say it again: whatever pit you're in, whatever weight you're carrying, whatever regret you're wrestling with, bring it to Jesus. He can handle it. He's not scared of your mess. He's not put off by your past. He's not mad at you. He's reaching for you.

Take His hand.

You don't have to climb out alone. You don't have to prove anything. Just come.

If you haven't already, I want to invite you to ask the Lord to come into your life. You don't need perfect words, just a sincere heart. If you're ready, pray this simple prayer with me:

Dear Heavenly Father, I believe in Your Son Jesus Christ. I believe that He died on the cross for my sins and that He rose from the grave, and that I am forgiven. Help me to walk with You. Thank You for saving me. In Jesus' name, Amen.

If you prayed that prayer and meant it, the Bible says you are saved (Romans 10:9). You are a new creation. Welcome home.

I used to live without knowing Him.

I don't do that anymore.

The first step toward a successful recovery is brutal honesty.

Chapter 9: Help is Out There: How Teens Can Talk to Parents, Friends, or Counselors About Addiction

You might know the name Demi Lovato. Famous singer, former Disney star, and someone who seemed to have it all: fame, talent, fans, a successful career. She was on stage, in magazines, and on red carpets. But what a lot of people didn't see was the storm she was facing behind the spotlight. Behind the polished image was a young person struggling with deep emotional pain.

Demi has shared openly that she began using substances as a way to numb that pain, to escape feelings she didn't know how to deal with. For a while, it worked. Or at least, it seemed to. But deep inside, the damage was building. The coping mechanism she thought was helping her stay afloat was actually pulling her under, little by little.

At just 18, Ms. Lovato checked into rehab for substance use and mental health struggles. That decision didn't come easily.

It came after denial, secrecy, fear, and shame. In interviews and documentaries, she's been brutally honest about how terrifying it was to ask for help.

She's talked about how she was afraid people would think less of her, that she would ruin her image, that she would be seen as weak or broken. She was afraid to let down the people who looked up to her. But in the end, she realized something critical: staying silent was more dangerous than speaking up. So she asked for help. That decision saved her life.

Her story is powerful because it reminds us that addiction doesn't care who you are. It doesn't matter how successful, smart, talented, or loved you might be; anyone can struggle with addiction. Anyone can rise again, even from the darkest places.

This chapter isn't about celebrities. It's about the quiet struggle, the kind that hides in plain sight. The late-night habits that started out as relief but now feel more like survival. The substances or screens or patterns you swore you were managing…until you weren't. It's about knowing something's wrong but not knowing where to start.

Maybe you're scared that if you say something, everything will fall apart. That people will be mad or upset with you. That you'll lose friends. That you'll be labeled or judged. That things will never be the same.

Asking for help isn't a surrender, it's a turning point. This chapter is about what it looks like to begin again with purpose and direction.

Understanding the Warning Signs

You don't have to be passed out, arrested, or
at rock bottom to have a problem. Addiction
often starts small.

Harmless. Manageable. Until it isn't. Maybe it's a drink at a party, a pill from a friend, or vaping to take the edge off. At first, it feels like no big deal. Then, slowly, it becomes a habit. Then a pattern. Then, before you know it, it's the only way you know how to get through the day.

You might still be functioning and doing what needs to be done each day. But something inside you knows. You can feel it. Maybe you're using just to feel normal. Maybe you get anxious or on edge when you can't. Maybe you've started crossing lines you swore you never would. And now, part of you wishes you never started. Or wonders if it's time to stop. Like you've gone farther down this road than you ever meant to. That uneasy feeling that something isn't right is worth paying attention to. The quiet voice telling you this might be slipping out of your control is too.

So how do you know if it's actually a problem?

Here are a few early signs that you might be slipping:

- Using substances to deal with stress, sadness, or anger
- Hiding your use from friends or family
- Lying about where you are or what you're doing
- Losing interest in stuff you used to love
- Spending more time with people who push boundaries or take big risks

- Finding it harder to focus or feel excited about anything unless you're high or buzzed
- Feeling like you need it just to feel okay, not even to feel good
- Planning your daily activities around your drinking

It's not just about how much or how often you're using, it's about why you're using and what it's doing to you. If it's becoming your go-to coping method, if it's starting to replace people or passions you once cared about, that's a red flag.

Quick Self-Check: "Am I Losing Control?"

- Have I tried to cut back and failed?
- Am I using more than I meant to?
- Do I feel nervous or anxious when I can't get it?
- Am I making decisions I regret while under the influence?
- Is it getting harder to hide this from people?
- Do I feel like I wouldn't know how to get through the the day or the week without it?

If you answered yes to a few of these, that doesn't make you a bad person, it just means it's time to talk to someone. These are early warning signs, and recognizing them now gives you the power to turn things around. You don't need a diagnosis or a disaster to reach out. You just need the courage to be honest and to say, "I don't want this for my life." That one insight, that moment of clarity, is your opportunity, your wake-up call. It is the perfect reason to speak up.

Why It's So Hard to Ask for Help

We don't grow up being taught how to say: "I need help." Most of us are told to be strong, figure it out, or just deal. We learn to downplay our emotions, to wear a smile when we feel like crying, and to act like we're fine even when we're clearly not. Vulnerability isn't something we're often encouraged to show, especially when we're hurting, and especially if you are a male.

Asking for help can feel like admitting failure, even though it's the opposite. It means admitting that something isn't working. It can feel scary.

Let's name the fears that might be holding you back:

Fear of getting in trouble

Maybe you're afraid of being grounded, losing privileges, or having your phone taken away. If you're older, it may be losing a job or a relationship. Or maybe it's bigger than that, the fear that speaking up will change how people see you. That it'll create tension, disappointment, or consequences you can't undo. Sometimes it feels safer to stay quiet than to risk breaking something you're barely holding together.

Shame

It's not just fear of being judged, it's the fear that once people know, they'll never see you the same way again. That they'll think you're weak, broken, or somehow less than you were. Maybe you're afraid that someone will think something is wrong with you. Shame can make you feel like you're the only one dealing with this, like your struggle is a stain you have to hide. But you're not the only one. And you're not damaged.

Thinking you can fix it alone

You tell yourself you've got this. If you just cut back, stay disciplined, stay quiet, you'll get it under control. No one ever has to find out. But deep down, you know it's not really working. You're white-knuckling it. The longer you go without help, the heavier it gets. Wanting to do it alone doesn't make you strong. It makes you human. But reaching out is what actually helps you heal.

Believing no one will understand.

Maybe you've tried to open up before and got brushed off. Or you've seen how others react to people who struggle and it wasn't kind. It's easy to believe that if you speak up, you'll be dismissed, judged, or told you're exaggerating. So you keep it inside, afraid of being misunderstood. But the right people will listen. You just have to find them.

Peer pressure

When everyone else seems fine with it, or even proud of it, it's hard to admit you're not. It can feel like you're the only one questioning the party, the habit, the risk. Like speaking up will make you the outsider. But real strength isn't about going along, it's about being honest with and to yourself, even if no one else is ready to be.

Here's something important to remember: Fears shrink when you face them. And the people who truly care about you will care even more when you're honest. They'll respect you for having the courage to speak up.

It's okay to feel scared. It's okay to hesitate. But don't let fear keep you stuck or hold you back. Behind that fear is freedom, the freedom to be seen, heard, and helped. Pushing through the fear is what leads to healing.

The Power of Speaking Up

Asking for help is a power move. It's a declaration that you're no longer willing to carry the weight alone. It means you're stepping out of the shadows and choosing truth over silence. It's easy to feel like vulnerability is weakness, but it's actually the most courageous thing you can do.

Asking for help is not an admission of failure. It's an act of strength. It says, "I want more for myself. I want to feel better. I'm ready for something different." That's bravery. That takes real courage. For me, it took faith, too.

You don't have to wait for a complete collapse to deserve help. You don't have to crash your life into pieces to justify reaching out. Most people who've been through recovery will tell you they wish they'd asked sooner. The longer you wait, the harder it can feel, but the truth is, it's never too early, and it's never too late.

Support doesn't come with strings or conditions. It comes with open hands, listening ears, and people who've either been where you are or who care enough to walk with you through it.

Healing doesn't begin with perfection. It begins with one brave sentence. Once you say, "I need help," you unlock a whole new chapter of possibility.

You don't have to know the whole path yet. You just have to be willing to take the first step.

This is the most important part of this chapter. You're ready to talk, but where do you start? Who do you go to? What if they don't get it?

The good news is you have options. There isn't one "right" person to talk to. What matters is that you start the conversation somewhere. With someone. Once you do, the burden starts to lift immediately.

Trusted Adults

Sometimes, the safest place to begin is with someone who already knows you. Someone who has seen you grow up, who has invested in your life, and who genuinely cares, whether they show it perfectly or not.

- *Parent or guardian*: This can be the hardest person to go to, especially if you're afraid of disappointing them. But many parents would rather know and help than be left in the dark. Even if their first reaction is shock or anger, it usually comes from fear. Fear of losing you. Fear of not knowing how to help. Underneath that, love still lives there.
- *School counselor*: They're not just there for academic stress or class schedules. School counselors are trained to support emotional and behavioral health, and they often know about resources you didn't even know existed.

- *Coach or teacher*: You might not think they'd understand, but many have seen students walk this path before. A trusted adult at school can be a powerful ally, and sometimes it's easier to talk to someone who isn't family.
- *Family friend or relative*: Someone who knows you but isn't in your everyday orbit might be a great first listener. They may help you think clearly and offer guidance without the intensity of someone closer.

Professional Resources

You might feel more comfortable talking to someone completely outside your personal life. That's totally okay. Sometimes it's easier to be honest with someone who doesn't already know your story.

- *Therapist or counselor*: Look for a licensed mental health professional—especially one who specializes in teens or addiction. They can help you talk through what you're feeling, offer coping strategies, and connect you to more help if needed.
- *Doctor or nurse*: Medical professionals aren't there to judge. If you're honest, they can guide you toward safe recovery options. Legally, they're bound by confidentiality laws (with a few exceptions involving safety).
- *Helplines*: If talking in person feels too scary at first, try a helpline. These are anonymous, confidential, and available 24/7:
- *SAMHSA National Helpline* (24/7, free & confidential): 1-800-662-HELP (4357)

- *Veterans and Military Crisis Line*: Call or Text 988
- *Crisis Text Line*: Text HOME or HELLO to 741741 to connect with a trained crisis counselor anytime
- *Teen Line* (peer-to-peer support): Text TEEN to 839863 (6 PM–9 PM PST); Call 800-852-8336 (6 PM–10 PM PST)

Using the Internet to Find Help

Your phone or laptop can become a powerful recovery tool. Searching "addiction help for..." might feel weird or scary, but it can open doors for you.

- *FindTreatment.gov*: A government-run directory where you can enter your zip code and see treatment centers near you.
- *7 Cups*: A free online platform where you can talk to trained listeners or licensed therapists in real-time.
- *Reddit* (with caution): Communities like r/stopdrinking, r/leaves (for weed), and r/addiction provide anonymous, real stories and encouragement. Just be mindful, online spaces can be unfiltered, so look for supportive, non-toxic voices.
- *YouTube, Instagram, TikTok* and other reels: Some creators share raw, honest stories about recovery. Hearing someone else say "I've been there too" can make you feel less alone. Just be sure to follow people who are real about the hard parts, not glamorizing use.

Peer Support

Never underestimate the power of talking to someone your own age who gets it. Even if they're not a professional, they might offer understanding, hope, or even help you take the next step.

- *A trusted friend*: If there's someone who's noticed something's off, or who's already said, "Are you okay?," consider opening up. You don't have to tell them everything, just enough to not feel alone.
- *Teen recovery groups*: Some communities (and many websites) host youth-focused recovery groups. These might be 12-step (like Teen AA) or more casual and peer-based. Some are local; many are virtual.
- *Youth programs or centers*: Community centers, religious organizations, and nonprofits sometimes offer safe spaces where teens can talk without judgment.

How to Start the Conversation

The words don't have to be perfect. They just have to be true.

Here are some real, simple ways to begin:

- "I think I need help with something, and I don't know how to say it."
- "I've been doing something I'm not proud of, and I don't want it to get worse."
- "I feel like things are getting out of control, and I don't want to keep hiding it."
- "Can I talk to you about something that's been hard for me?"

- "I don't want this in my life anymore, but I don't know how to change it."

If saying it out loud feels too intense, that's okay. You don't have to have the perfect words. You can start small. You can text. You can write a note. You can send an email. You can say:

- "Can we talk later? I'm struggling."
- "I don't know how to say this, but I need help."
- "Something's been weighing on me and I don't want to carry it alone anymore."

You can even just say, "Can you check in on me later?" or send a song, a meme, or a quote that gets the message across. It doesn't have to be a full explanation. It just has to be real. That one small reach can be the beginning of everything changing.

You don't have to tell everything all at once. You just need to take the lid off the silence. Once you do, it becomes easier to breathe.

What You Can Expect When You Ask for Help

Opening up about something this personal can feel like standing at the edge of a cliff. You brace yourself for rejection, judgment, or disappointment. You imagine people pulling away, getting angry, or shutting down.

But more often than not, the opposite happens.

People lean in. They listen. They care.

They may not always show it perfectly, but underneath the initial reaction is usually concern, not judgment. You might expect anger, but what you'll often see is relief. Gratitude. A sense that they're glad you finally said something out loud.

People who care about you will want to support you, not punish you. Whether it's a partner, a parent, a friend, a teacher, or a boss, most people don't want to see you struggle. Asking for help gives them a chance to stand beside you instead of watching you suffer in silence.

Some may cry. Some may go quiet. Some won't know what to say at first. That's okay. The most important thing is that you've started the conversation.

And yes, sometimes the first person you tell won't respond well. That doesn't mean you were wrong to speak up. It just means you might need to try again. The right help is out there. You are allowed to ask more than once. In fact, asking again takes courage. It means you're serious about taking care of yourself.

You're not alone in this. You're not the first person to reach a breaking point or realize something has to change. But you're doing something powerful, you're choosing not to stay silent. That one decision will change everything.

Common Fears, Real Answers

"Will the people I love be angry?"
They might be shocked, scared, or overwhelmed, but those emotions usually come from love, not hate. Most people, especially family and close friends, want to see you safe and well. The moment may be hard, but their love doesn't disappear.

"Will I get in trouble at work or school?"

In most cases, organizations are required to offer support, not just consequences. Many schools and workplaces have programs or people in place to help with mental health and substance-related challenges. Reaching out doesn't mean you're weak, it means you're taking responsibility.

"Will people label me or see me differently forever?"

Some might, for a moment. But people grow. You grow. You are not defined by what you're going through. You're defined by how you face it. Asking for help doesn't put a label on you; it opens a door to something better.

"Will I lose relationships?"

You might. And that can hurt. But it also reveals who's really in your corner. The people who truly care about you will stay. Over time, you'll find new people who understand, who respect your honesty, and who want to walk with you, not away from you.

A Path Forward

Once you say the words out loud, something begins to shift. The pressure, the secrecy, the fear, it doesn't disappear overnight, but it becomes lighter. You're no longer carrying it alone. That moment of honesty is the beginning of change.

You might be connected with a school counselor who listens without judgment. You might meet with a therapist who helps you make sense of what you're feeling and why. You might just start being more honest with someone close to you, a parent, a coach, a sibling, a friend. No matter how small that first conversation feels, it matters. It creates momentum.

Recovery isn't instant. There will be good days and hard days. There might be moments when you feel stronger than ever, and moments when you wonder if you're strong enough to keep going. But now you'll have support. You'll have tools. You'll have people walking with you. And you'll have someone to help hold you accountable to your own words.

Slowly, step by step, the thing that once felt impossible becomes something you can face. The same way a fog lifts one layer at a time, clarity and confidence begin to return.

You don't need to map out the rest of your life to take the next right step. Just focus on today. On the choice in front of you. Every step forward counts. Every honest conversation is a win. Every day you choose to care for yourself is part of your healing.

The path ahead isn't about being perfect. It's about being real. It's about learning new ways to cope, building healthier habits, and proving to yourself, day by day, that you are more than what you've been through.

You're not behind. You're not broken. You're just at the beginning of something better.

Action Steps
Here's what you can do right now:

- Write down three people you could talk to. Don't overthink it. Just make a list of anyone you trust, even a little.
- Draft a short script or message. If you're not ready to say it out loud, write what you'd want to say. Get the words out of your head and onto paper or screen.
- Call a helpline anonymously. Even if it's just to practice. You're not committing to anything, just having a conversation.
- Search online for support. Look for recovery stories, peer groups, or mental health tools. The internet has real help. Use it wisely.
- Set a time and place. Choose when and how you'll talk to someone. After school, during a walk, in the car, on your lunch break, whatever feels safe.
- Write a simple "future self" manifesto. Nothing fancy. Just a few lines about what you want your life to look like in 3 months, 6 months, and one year. Be honest. Be specific. Let it remind you what you're moving toward. And let your words and actions create your future.

This isn't about fixing everything today. It's about opening the door. One step is enough to start. One voice is enough to break the silence.

Closing Encouragement

You are not broken. You are not alone. You are not past the point of help.

There are people in your life who care. People who will listen. People who want you to succeed. You might not have met them all yet, but they're out there. The moment you reach out, you move one step closer to finding them.

Some people go years without saying a word. Not you. You're choosing a different path. One built on truth, healing, and strength.

"You can change your future with one brave moment."

Someday, not long from now, you'll be able to say those words with peace, power, and pride:

"I don't do that anymore."

You don't have to have the perfect words. You can start small.

Chapter 10: When It's Your Kid— A Parent's Guide

There's nothing that breaks you faster than watching your child slip away. Not physically, but in every other way that matters. You see it in their eyes. You hear it in their voice. You feel it in the space between you, growing wider by the day. They lie. You pretend to believe them. And all the while, you're losing them, and it seems there's nothing you can do to stop it.

Addiction doesn't care how good a parent you are. It doesn't care how many rules you set, how many bedtime stories you read, how many games you drove them to, or how much you love them. It comes for families that did everything right. Like a thief in the night, with no mercy and no warning.

First, it steals the laughter from your kitchen. Then the peace from your home. Family dinners are replaced with slammed doors, awkward silences, and conversations that feel like walking through a minefield. You start to second-guess everything. Your parenting, your instincts, your memories of who your kid used to be.

If you're reading this chapter, maybe you already suspect something. Or maybe you already know. Maybe your kid is smoking weed every day. Maybe you found pills. Maybe they came home slurring words and smelling like alcohol.

Or maybe you haven't caught them yet, but your gut is screaming at you to pay attention.

Listen to that feeling or intuition. It's not paranoia. It's not overreacting. It's the part of you that knows your kid. When something feels off, it probably is.

Maybe you're exhausted from pretending everything's fine. Maybe you're lying awake at night, running worst-case scenarios. Maybe you're grieving the version of your child you used to know, and no one's permitting you to say that out loud.

Parenting through addiction is a kind of heartbreak no one prepares you for. You feel helpless, angry, terrified, and still, somehow, hopeful. Deep down, you believe they're still in there. And you're right. They are. Under the fear, the lies, and the wreckage. That's what keeps you going.

So let's talk about it. Parent to parent. Human to human. This is hard. Really hard. I'm sorry you're here. But I'm glad you are.

First: Let's Kill the Shame

Parents get hit with shame the second this kind of thing shows up.

What did I do wrong?
Where did I mess up?

How could they do this after everything I've given them?

Listen. None of us are perfect. We lose our patience. We mess up. We get it wrong sometimes.

But this isn't your fault. Addiction isn't your fault.

Your kid didn't start using because you didn't make enough family dinners. They started because they were hurting, or lost, or trying to get away from something. Maybe even peer pressure. But, whatever it was, using felt like a way out.

Maybe they were bullied. Maybe they have anxiety they never told you about. Maybe they watched you, or someone else, struggle and didn't know how to talk about it. Maybe they just wanted to feel okay, even for a little while. That's not your failure. That's them trying to survive.

Shame will shut you down. Make you quiet. Make you believe no one else could possibly understand.

But you're not the only one.

Plenty of families are living this behind closed doors. The ones who look fine in public. Who smile for photos. Who show up to church, and then go home to the same fear and chaos you're dealing with.

It's okay to feel wrecked. To be angry. To not know what to do. Just don't go silent.

This isn't about blame. It's about telling the truth. Staying in it. Not backing out when it gets ugly and tough.

You're still standing. So is your kid.
That means there's still something to fight for.

Real Story: Even Him

Robert Downey Jr. is a very familiar name. Millions of people know him as Iron Man, or from one of a dozen other blockbuster roles.

But before all that, he was a teenager drowning in addiction.

His father, also an actor, introduced him to drugs when he was just eight years old. Not maliciously, just carelessly. A shared joint. A normalized habit. And from there, it spiraled.

Downey grew up acting in films while secretly battling a growing dependency. As he got older, it got darker. He cycled through arrests, rehabs, and jail time. He was in and out so often, people assumed he was a lost cause.

His parents watched it unfold. They loved him. They hurt. And for years, nothing seemed to work.

But the story didn't end there.

Eventually, with real support, real boundaries, and his own decision to fight, he came back. He got sober. He rebuilt his life. And now, he's more than just a movie star. He's a father. A husband. A living reminder that even the most messed-up story can still turn around.

His journey doesn't erase the pain his family went through. But it proves something important: Your kid is not too far gone.

No matter how far they've fallen, if there's still breath in their lungs, they can turn things around.

Addiction doesn't care if you're rich or famous. It doesn't care how talented your kid is.

Recovery doesn't care either. It doesn't need a perfect past.

It just needs someone who hasn't given up and is willing to take the next right step toward something better.

Be that person. Even when it's hard. Especially when it's hard.

Sometimes the kid everyone gave up on becomes the one who inspires everyone else to hold on.

The Warning Signs

Substance use doesn't always look like someone passed out or getting arrested.

Sometimes it looks like:

- A sudden change in friends
- Always asking for money
- Skipping school or dropping grades
- Sleeping too much, or hardly at all
- Getting defensive over small things
- Pulling away from family
- Red eyes, strange behavior, or weird smells
- Lies. Lots of lies.

And it's not always obvious. It creeps in slowly, just like fog does.

Maybe they laugh less, snap more, avoid eye contact. Maybe they're always gone, or locked in their room. Maybe you've caught them in lies that don't add up, but you brush them off because you want to believe it's nothing.

Some of this can look like normal teen stuff. But deep down, you know when something's off. That inner voice? That's your gut. Trust it.

You know your kid. You know their rhythms, their tells. When your gut starts lighting up like a dashboard, listen. You don't need proof. You need courage.

It's better to speak up too soon than to wait too long.

You're not accusing. You're caring. You're paying attention.

And if you're wrong? They still know you love them.

If you're right? You might catch it before it's too late.

Either way, it matters.

How to Talk to Them

This is where many parents struggle, not because they don't care, but because they don't know how to approach the conversation. They're scared. Hurt. Angry. And it comes out sideways.

You find something suspicious, and suddenly you're yelling, making threats, or crying while your kid goes blank. Maybe they argue. Maybe they walk away. Either way, you feel like you made it worse.

Here's what doesn't work:

- Screaming
- Threatening
- Shaming
- Begging
- "If you loved me, you wouldn't do this."

Even when those reactions come from love, they sound like judgment. And kids who are hiding won't respond to pressure; they'll shut down.

So what does work?

Staying calm. Speaking clearly. Letting them know you love them, no matter what. That you're here, through the good and the bad. That you're here, and they don't have to face it alone.

Try:

"I've noticed some things that don't feel right. I love you too much to ignore them."

"This isn't about getting you in trouble. I just want to understand."

"I'm scared, and I want to help. But I need you to be honest."

Then stop talking. Seriously. Let the silence stretch. Let them lie if they need to. You're planting a seed, not trying to win the conversation.

Even if they walk away, roll their eyes, or say nothing, they heard you.

You're saying: "I see you. I care. I'm not going anywhere."

This is what love with boundaries looks like:

"I don't like what you're doing, but I still love you."

"You're always safe here, even if you don't like what I say."

"If you want help, I'll walk with you."

You're not a doormat. You're not ignoring the problem. You're being the safest person in the room when their world feels like it's falling apart.

And if they won't talk? That's okay. Don't force it. Just keep showing up.

Watch their favorite show with them. Go out to eat, or Jamba, or coffee. Write them a note. Encourage time with a mentor or counselor. Keep the door open, without shoving them through it.

Connection is the goal. Addiction isolates. Connection heals.

Don't expect to fix everything in one talk. This is about building a bridge and being willing to stand on it until they're ready to cross.

You may need to have the same talk ten different times. You might feel like nothing is working. But love with boundaries echoes in the background, and when they hit their bottom, they'll remember who stood by them.

So don't scream.
Don't threaten.
Don't throw their whole future in their face.

Stand firm. Speak truth. Love hard, with limits.

And when it all blows up, because it might, give yourself grace.

You're going to mess up. Say the wrong thing. Break down in tears.

That doesn't mean you're failing.

That means you're in the fight.

It's a fight worth fighting, and there's no easy way out.

What You Can Do

You can't force your kid to stop using. I wish there was a magic sentence, a consequence, something that could snap them out of it. But addiction doesn't respond to logic, guilt, or even love. It feeds on pain and denial.

Still, that doesn't mean you're powerless.

You shape the environment. You set the tone. You decide what kind of parent you'll be in the storm. You can't control them, but you can control how you respond.

Get help. For them and for you.

You don't have to figure this out alone. You're too close to it, and that's normal.

Start with a therapist, counselor, pediatrician, or addiction specialist. If your kid won't go, you still can. Learn how to respond instead of react. Learn how to set boundaries that stick. Learn how to breathe again.

And don't underestimate the power of a support group. AA, Al-Anon, SMART Recovery, Family & Friends, or even a local parent circle. Just simply hearing "me too" from someone who's been in your shoes before can help you stay grounded and help pull you through.

Set boundaries. And hold them.

Boundaries aren't punishments, they're safety measures.

"If you're using, you can't stay out all night."

"If drugs show up in this house, there will be consequences."

"We'll support your recovery, not your using."

Say what you mean. Mean what you say. Don't bluff. Don't backpedal.

Will they push against it? Of course. That's part of it. But clarity and consistency are more powerful than any punishment.

Let the consequences happen.

This one hurts. Because every part of you wants to protect them. But protecting them from pain often protects them from growth.

If they mess up, don't cover it. If they flunk out or get caught, let it stand. Pain can be a turning point if we stop cushioning every fall. It is a wonderful opportunity for growth.

You can still be there. Not to fix it, but to say, "I'm here. I love you. What do we do now?"

Encourage anything that isn't the substance.

Recovery isn't just about saying no, it's about finding something worth saying yes to.

If they want to work out, hike, bake, volunteer, or just grab coffee, say yes. Support anything that brings joy, connection, or purpose.

These aren't distractions. They're signs of life. Every laugh, every effort, every sober moment is a small win. Celebrate them.

Take care of yourself. Seriously.

This can consume you if you're not careful. You still have needs. You still matter. Take care of your own mental health, body, and soul.

You can't parent well if you're running on fumes. Rest. Eat. Move. Talk to someone. Let yourself grieve, breathe, and be human.

They don't need you to be perfect. They need you to be whole.

What Not to Do

Some of this you've probably already done. That's okay. No judgment, just a reset. You're learning in real time, under pressure, in the middle of a storm. Give yourself some grace. But if you want to be a steady force in your kid's recovery, you've got to start showing up differently.

Here's what doesn't help, even when it feels right:

1. Don't make it about you.

Yes, you're hurt. Yes, you're scared. But if every conversation becomes *how could you do this to me*, they'll shut down. They're already drowning in shame. They don't need more guilt.

If they feel like the villain in your story, they'll either run, or lie even better. This isn't about centering your pain. It's about helping them stay connected through theirs.

2. Don't rescue every time.

You can't absorb their consequences. You can't soften every blow. And if you keep trying, you'll delay the moment that could change everything.

Pain isn't punishment. Sometimes it's the only thing strong enough to break denial. Let it do what it needs to do. Be there when it hits, not to fix it, but to say, "This is hard. What now?"

3. Don't let love turn into enabling.

There's a thin line between support and enabling. One leads to growth. The other keeps them stuck.

Love says, "I'm here." Enabling says, "I'll fix it so you don't have to face it."

You can love your kid and still say no. That's not cruelty. That's clarity. Which might be exactly what they need in that moment.

4. Don't wait for it to go away.

It's tempting to hope this is just a phase. But addiction doesn't fade with silence. It grows deeper.

Don't wait for a disaster. Don't wait for the arrest or the overdose or the hospital visit. Trust your gut. Speak the truth early. It's the best chance you've got.

5. Don't isolate.
It's easy to pull back. You're too tired to explain, too ashamed to ask for help.

But isolation won't help you. It just makes things harder.

You don't need a crowd. Just one or two people who get it, won't flinch, and who can sit with the hard stuff and remind you that you're not crazy, and you're not alone.

Bottom line? You don't have to be perfect. You just have to be present. Show up. Say the hard thing. Let them sit in the discomfort of their choices. And remind them over and over again, they're not too far gone to come home.

The Long Game
When it comes to addiction, there isn't a one-time talk or a dramatic intervention that fixes everything. It's not neat. It's not fast. It's a long, winding road, fought one day, one hour, one minute at a time.

There will be setbacks. Moments when you think you're making progress, only to watch it unravel. That's not failure. That's recovery. It's not a straight line, it zigzags. Some days, the win is them going to a meeting. Other days, it's just them coming home.

Your job? Hold the line.

Love them. Set boundaries. Stay consistent. Even when you're tired. Even when it feels helpless. Even when they push you away.

Your steady presence might be the one thing they come back to when everything else falls apart.

You need to remember that their recovery is not your responsibility. You didn't cause it. You can't control it. And you can't carry it for them.

But you can show up. With clarity. With compassion. With strength. You can love them without losing yourself. And when they fall, you can say, "I'm here, but the choice to rise is still yours."

This is slow, painful work. But when they come back, it won't be because you fixed everything. It'll be because you kept loving them through it all, even when they couldn't love themselves.

Don't Forget Yourself

You matter, too.

It's easy to disappear into your child's crisis. To stop sleeping, cancel plans, lie to your friends, and pretend you're fine when you're falling apart inside.

Don't.

You're not just a parent, you're a human being with limits. Get your own therapist. Join a support group. Talk to someone who understands. You don't have to carry this alone.

And if you're always the one who takes care of everyone else? Consider this your wake-up call: you can't help them if you're drowning too.

You're allowed to cry. To scream. To admit this is breaking your heart.

You're allowed to breathe.

Encourage Everything

If your kid wants to go to a game instead of getting high, say yes. If they want to bake something, take a walk, or sign up for a class. Encourage it.

You're looking for sparks of life. Glimpses of who they are beneath the addiction.

Even if it seems small. Even if it doesn't last. Celebrate it.

It is those kinds of tiny steps that are the foundation recovery is built on.

When You Feel Like Giving Up

You will have days when you're done. Burnt out. Numb. Tired of the lies. The chaos. The fear. You'll wonder if anything you're doing is making a difference.

Here's what I'll tell you: it is.

Even if they're still using. Even if they're not ready. Your love still matters. Your presence matters. Your boundaries matter.

You don't have to fix it all. Just keep showing up—with truth, and with love.

Sometimes recovery starts with a memory:

"My mom never stopped believing in me."

"My dad didn't walk away."

"That one thing they said—I couldn't shake it."

Your love might be the only thing that sticks when everything else falls apart.

What Recovery Really Looks Like

It's not instant. Not loud. Not perfect. It is long term, hard work, and the most valuable thing you will ever own.

It looks like:

- One honest conversation
- One boundary held
- One sober night
- One therapist session they didn't cancel
- One apology
- One moment where they chose truth

That's what healing is. Stack enough of those moments, and they start to build something new.

Relapses may happen. That doesn't erase progress. It just means there's still more work to do.

But if they're still breathing, there's still hope.

And if you're still showing up, there's still a fight to be fought. And if love is still present, there's still something to build on.

Closing Words: You're Not Alone

This stuff is hard. But you can do it.

Loving someone through addiction might be the hardest thing you'll ever face. It's confusing. Exhausting. Heartbreaking. But you're still here. Still showing up. Still fighting. It might not feel like that matters, but it does.

No, this isn't the story you wanted. You didn't sign up for this. But this is the chapter you're in. And how you show up here shapes everything.

You don't need all the answers. You won't get it right every time. You just have to keep going. One day at a time.

Keep loving.
Keep holding the line.
Keep asking for help.
Keep speaking truth, even when your voice shakes.

You might feel invisible. Like none of it's working. But your kid notices, more than they let on. Even if they don't say it. Even if they push you away. Deep down, they know: you haven't quit on them.

And when they're ready to come back, they'll remember.

So don't give up.

Don't believe the lie that says it's too late.

I Don't Do That Anymore

Don't underestimate what your presence means.

You're still in the fight.

I used to be too proud to ask for help.

I don't do that anymore.

Chapter 11: From MVP to Oxy

I got injured during the spring game at Montana State. At the time, I didn't know it would be the last play of my career. I didn't get carted off with a dramatic goodbye. I didn't get a farewell season or one last carry. I just got hurt, went home for surgery, and never made it back. One chapter closed, and I didn't even realize I was already on the last page.

After surgery, the doctor handed me a prescription for painkillers. It was standard procedure. Just a little something to help with the pain. I never filled it. I didn't even go to the pharmacy. I knew what those pills could do, not just to my body, but to my life.

My family has a history with addiction, and that fear lived close enough to the surface that I didn't want to take the risk. I stuck with Tylenol instead. It didn't make the recovery easier, but it was what I thought was best for me.

That choice kept me off one path, but it didn't stop me from going down another.

Just because I didn't take the pills doesn't mean I didn't try to escape. I turned to alcohol, as you're aware of by now at this point in the book. It became my way of coping once the structure was gone and the silence got too loud.

In moments like that, when your career ends sooner than expected, when the structure and identity you've known for years basically disappear overnight, it's easy to want relief from more than just the physical pain. It's not just your body that hurts. It's your pride. Your sense of purpose. Your place in the world.

For a lot of athletes, the silence that follows
an injury or an exit from the game is so loud,
they'll take almost anything to drown it out.

I remember feeling completely lost in the weeks after my injury. I didn't know what to do with myself. The routines were gone. The adrenaline, the competition, the team, all of it.

In their place was this strange emptiness I didn't know how to fill. I could have gone down the same road I'd seen others take. A few pills to take the edge off. A few more to sleep. Before you know it, you're chasing the feeling more than the relief. And then it's not about healing anymore, it's about escaping.

The Slippery Slope of Toughness

That path doesn't always start with pills. Sometimes it starts with the injections. Cortisone. Toradol. Steroids. Whatever it takes to get back on the field. They tell you it's just a temporary solution. They say, "This will reduce the swelling," or "This will get you through this game." As a competitor, you tell yourself it's just one more thing you have to do to compete.

But those injections can mask serious damage. They keep you moving, but they don't help you heal. They teach you to ignore your body's signals, to override your limits. And once you start overriding pain, it becomes a habit you don't even question.

According to a 2022 NCAA report, nearly 23% of college athletes report misusing prescription medications, including opioids. That number climbs when you look at athletes dealing with long-term or repeat injuries.

The U.S. Centers for Disease Control and Prevention (CDC) estimates that athletes are up to 50% more likely than non-athletes to be prescribed opioids, especially in high-contact sports like football, wrestling, and hockey. For many, the line between use and misuse isn't clear. It's not about getting high, it's about getting through.

The Culture of Playing Through Pain

For student-athletes, this risk is even more pronounced. Most of us start playing when we're kids. We learn discipline through practice. We find identity in our role on the team. We get used to pushing through pain and being rewarded for toughness. Coaches talk about heart and grit and playing through the injury if you can walk.

Somewhere along the line, pain stops being something to notice. It becomes something to ignore, something you fight through, something you get patched up for so you can get back on the field.

It's no wonder so many of us don't even realize how bad it is until it's too late.

There's a culture in sports that doesn't just tolerate pain, it celebrates it. You get praised for playing hurt. You get respect for keeping quiet and grinding through it.

But, when the game is over, whether because of injury or age or life circumstances, all that toughness leaves you with is a bunch of untreated wounds, physical, emotional, and mental, that no one trained you how to deal with.

Painkillers become the shortcut. The easy answer. The coach doesn't have to bench you. The trainer doesn't have to tell you to sit out. You don't have to face the reality that maybe you're not invincible. You just pop a pill and get back to work. Until one day, you can't get through the day without it.

When Everything Becomes Too Much

I knew guys who got hurt and did everything by the book. Surgery, rehab, the medications the doctors prescribed, but somewhere along the way, something shifted. You'd see it in their eyes. The light started to dim a little. They were slower to laugh, quicker to anger, more distant in conversations. It didn't happen all at once, but it was noticeable if you were paying attention, which most people weren't.

They didn't disappear from the roster, but they did start to disappear from themselves. Come to think of it, a few of them actually did disappear from the roster. Injuries turned into setbacks. Setbacks turned into silence. You'd stop seeing them at workouts. They'd miss meetings or start hanging on the edge of the group, quieter than usual. They were still there, physically, but something in them had shifted. Scholarships and dreams were lost because of it.

They weren't trying to get high. They were just trying to survive and keep their dreams alive. At first, it was about recovery. About staying in the game. But then it became about something else: trying to feel normal, trying to find a sense of control in a life that suddenly felt unfamiliar.

They were chasing something steady, something that made sense. They were trying to escape the confusion that comes when the only version of yourself you've ever known suddenly stops existing.

The Identity Crisis

When the uniform comes off, who remains?

No one teaches you how to stop being an athlete. No one prepares you for the identity crisis that comes after your last whistle is blown. For all of the high-level athletes I have ever met or played with, it was all we ever knew and dreamed of since we were kids. It was who we were. Or so we thought.

I think about people like Ryan Leaf. He was the second overall pick in the NFL Draft in 1998. Had all the potential in the world. But with the pressure, the expectations, and the injuries, things started to spiral.

One night in Las Vegas, he took a few pills. He's talked openly about how that moment changed everything, not just because of the physical relief, but because of what those pills did to his mental state.

For the first time in a long time, he felt like he could escape. Escape the headlines. Escape the disappointment. Escape the constant reminders that he hadn't lived up to the hype. Being labeled a bust, being taunted by fans everywhere he went, it weighed on him more than people realized.

The pills dulled that pain. They made him feel like, just for a moment, he could breathe again. But that moment turned into a pattern, and that pattern turned into addiction.

Eventually, that path led him not just out of the league, but into prison. His story is heartbreaking, not because he failed to live up to expectations, but because the world never saw the emotional injuries he was carrying. The pills didn't just help with the injury. They helped numb the rest of it, too.

Now he speaks openly about addiction and recovery. His story is the kind of thing people need to hear.

Not every athlete goes pro, but a lot of them go through the same internal battle when their career ends. What do I do now? Who am I now, without the game that I love?

That's the real danger.

Addiction Isn't Always About Chasing A High

Sometimes addiction is about trying to recreate what you used to feel on the field. Focused. In control. Alive. Pills offer a shortcut to that feeling. For a little while, they quiet the noise and bring back a sense of certainty.

But when the routine disappears and the crowd stops cheering, that feeling gets harder to find. You start chasing it, not for the high, but for something that feels normal again. Something that fills the space where your identity used to live. Sometimes, that something is a pill. Or a bottle. Or some other drug.

The system doesn't help much, either. The pressure to perform starts young. College scholarships are on the line. Coaches are under pressure to win. Parents are invested, financially and emotionally. Trainers are expected to keep you on the field.

And when you're hurting, there's a line of people telling you to do whatever it takes to stay in the game. No one wants to be the one who can't play. No one wants to admit they're struggling.

So, the pills do their job, until they start doing too much.

There's also a mental health side to all of this that we don't talk about enough. The fear of failure. The anxiety around losing your spot. The depression that creeps in when you're sidelined. The identity crisis that hits when your season, or your career, is over.

We teach athletes how to push through pain, but we don't teach them how to process it. We celebrate comebacks, but we don't talk about the ones who don't make it back.

The Need for a New Kind of Toughness

Asking for help isn't a weakness. It's strength in its most honest form. You don't have to wait until you hit rock bottom to reach for a hand. You just have to decide you're done carrying it alone.

We need to normalize asking for help. We need to create space for athletes to say, "I'm not okay," without fear of being labeled weak. We need coaches, trainers and parents who are willing to prioritize a young person's well-being over the next win.

There are better ways to handle pain. Physical therapy. Mindfulness. Nutrition. Acupuncture.

There are athletes who've come back from major injuries without relying on pills, and their stories deserve to be told, too. When you only ever hear one version, the tough-it-out, take-the-meds, get-back-in-the-game version, you start to believe that's the only way.

But it's not.

Sometimes, recovery looks slower. It looks like missing a season. It looks like doing the hard work in a therapist's office instead of on a field. It looks like asking uncomfortable questions and making decisions other people don't understand. That takes a different kind of strength.

This isn't about blame or judgment. It's about awareness. About understanding the very real and often invisible pressures that athletes face when their identity is stripped away.

The truth is, a lot of good people fall into bad patterns, not because they're reckless, but because they're hurting and unsure of what else to do. It can happen fast. It can happen quietly. And by the time anyone notices, it can already feel too late.

This is a reminder that there's always a fork in the road, even if it doesn't look like one in the moment. It's easy to want the pain to stop. Easy to look for something that gives even a brief sense of relief.

There is another way, though, even when it feels like everything is falling apart.

So if you're reading this and you're in that space, post-injury, post-career, post-structure, and you're feeling that silence, that ache, that pressure to just feel normal again: pause. Talk to someone. Don't carry it alone. There are people who've been there. There are ways forward that don't involve numbing out. Life can still be full and meaningful, even without the game.

Your worth doesn't end when the game does. It took me time to see that, to believe there was still something valuable in me even after I stopped wearing the jersey. But it's true.

Who you are isn't just measured by stats, seasons, or what you used to do under stadium lights. There's life beyond the game, and it matters more than any score on a scoreboard ever will.

I used to believe that toughness meant staying silent. That pain was just part of the deal, and pushing through it was the only way to prove you belonged.

I used to think that if you weren't grinding, you were falling behind. I thought that choosing to rest or ask for help meant you didn't want it bad enough. I believed that the only way to stay in the game, on the field, and in life, was to power through everything, even when something inside you was breaking.

I don't do that anymore.

The Bigger Picture

These personal stories aren't isolated. They're part of a much larger pattern that deserves serious attention.

Opioid Use Among Student-Athletes

High School Students:

- Approximately 12.2% of U.S. high school students have reported using opioids, including prescription painkillers, at some point in their lives.

- High school athletes, especially those in high-contact sports like football, are at greater risk of being prescribed opioids for pain management, which increases the chances of misuse or long-term dependency.

College Student-Athletes:

- A 2023 NCAA study showed that 6% of student-athletes reported using narcotic pain medication with a prescription in the past year, down from 18% in 2013.

- 2% admitted to misusing narcotic pain medication.

- Research confirms that prescribed painkillers for injury treatment often become a gateway to more dangerous substances.

Alcohol Use in Athletic Culture

High School Athletes:

- A meta-analysis found that 78% of high school student-athletes reported lifetime alcohol use.

- Among team-sport athletes, 57% had consumed alcohol in the past month—compared to 45% of non-athletes.

College Athletes:

- College student-athletes report riskier patterns of alcohol consumption than their non-athlete peers.

- The NCAA's 2023 data showed 52% had consumed five or more drinks on multiple occasions in the last year.

- 11% acknowledged they needed help with alcohol-related issues.

- 33% of Division I collegiate athletes self-identified as experiencing symptoms of depression

---

*When the uniform
comes off,
who remains?*

Chapter 12: When Power and Addiction Meet— Struggles in the C-Suite

The Hidden Struggle

From the outside, the executive life looks like a dream job: the corner office, the travel, the nice dinners, the influence, the income. But behind the boardrooms and sales numbers, a lot of leaders are quietly struggling.

Addiction doesn't care how high your title is or how respected you are. In fact, the same traits that drive success, relentless focus, control, and the ability to power through, can also feed addiction, burnout, and self-destructive habits.

I've been in those rooms. Executive off-sites, post-conference dinners, closed-door meetings. I've seen shots poured during meetings and late-night implosions followed by quiet mornings. And I've heard that quiet voice inside ask, "Is this sustainable? Is this really who I want to be?"

No one talks about it. The higher you go, the less safe it feels.

Our quarterly trips were next-level. Fancy dinners, amazing seats at sporting events, everything paid for. The partner company had deep pockets and treated us like VIPs because we brought in big money. Open bars, extravagant meals, luxury hotels. The message was clear: this is your reward. You've earned it.

At first, it felt harmless. A drink to unwind. A toast at dinner. A nightcap back at the hotel. But before long, it turned into something else. A way to numb. A way to escape. A way to silence whatever was unsettled beneath the surface.

I watched smart, disciplined people slowly
start to drift. One compromise at a time.

They acted in ways they never would back home. But in that environment, it didn't just feel acceptable, it almost felt expected. Like this was the trade-off for the pressure we lived under. No one blinked. Everyone played along.

But it wasn't just the drinking that wore me down. It was the pretending. We were running on fumes, but we kept the show going. Laughing, smiling, raising glasses like nothing was wrong. Admitting you were struggling felt like breaking character.

Saying "I'm not okay" felt like surrender. And the more you climbed the ladder, the more you felt like you had to keep the mask on. You convince yourself the stress, the drinking, the burnout, that it's all just part of the job. Everyone's doing it. So you do too.

There were nights when things got blurry, when the energy crossed a line and the consequences lingered longer than the fun. You'd hear about something that happened, feel the tension the next morning, but no one really talked about it. We just moved on. Laughed it off. Kept the show going.

I had many mornings where I woke up with a hangover, foggy and drained, trying to shake off the night before. I'd get cleaned up, show up wherever I was supposed to, and play my part. That was the rhythm. That was success. Until it wasn't.

Eventually, it all starts to catch up. The pressure, the pace, the pretending, it wears you down. Things begin to crack where you thought you were solid. Once you finally see it for what it is, it never looks the same again.

That's when things begin to shift.

The Cost of Silence
Success can be lonely.

When you're in charge, you're expected to have answers. To stay calm. To deliver. So when something's off, when addiction or anxiety starts creeping in, you don't raise your hand. You shut your mouth and keep moving.

But hiding has a cost.

It affects how you make decisions. You react instead of think and respond. You avoid hard conversations. You send mixed signals to your team. At home, it's even worse. You check out. You snap. You try to numb the guilt or stress with more work, or more drinking. The breakdown doesn't always show up in the spreadsheets. It shows up in the moments you can't undo, too.

I've been there.

There were nights when we drank way too much. Nights when things were said that shouldn't have been said. When boundaries blurred, and behavior slipped. Still, we'd all show up the next morning, ironed and smiling like nothing happened. But underneath, things were broken.

We laughed it off. That was the deal, "We work hard, we play hard." But deep down, it didn't feel funny. It felt heavy. That quiet shame that sticks with you long after the buzz wears off.

The slide doesn't start with disaster. It starts small. You miss your workout one day. Then two. You silence a call from someone you shouldn't, then forget to call back. You start feeling irritated all the time. Sunday nights get heavier. Wins don't feel like wins.

You're still checking the boxes, but you're not really there. You start to lose the part of you that used to care. That used to feel. You keep showing up. Because that's what leaders do, right? You keep going. You push through. You hold it together.

That kind of strength can be misleading, though.

Real strength is stopping long enough to tell the truth about what's really going on. It's easy to keep playing along. It's harder to want more for yourself and to actually do something about it.

That's when you stop managing the image and start rebuilding the person.

I saw it happen to people who were smart, disciplined, and cared about their families. They didn't set out to lose their way—it just happened slowly. The pressure kept building, and the ways to escape were always within reach. I've seen careers stall out because someone couldn't stop drinking. I've seen marriages wear down under the weight of pretending everything was fine.

The worst part is that it's usually invisible, until it's not. Until there's a DUI. Until HR gets involved. Until a partner says they're done. Or until someone simply burns out, disappears, or breaks down.

I once watched a guy, someone I never really liked, but tolerated, get hammered, flirt aggressively, and take a woman back to his room. The next morning, he bragged about it over coffee like it was some kind of trophy. Whatever trace of respect I had for him disappeared instantly. He disgusted me. It's sad to say that I believe that kind of behavior isn't even rare.

Nobody calls it out. That's just how it goes. Keep your head down, play your role, pretend it's fine because that's what everyone else is doing.

Understanding the Drivers of Executive Addiction

This isn't just about alcohol or drugs. Most of the time, addiction in the executive world is about pressure. It's about trying to manage what's happening inside while keeping everything together on the outside. It's about avoiding what hurts and chasing whatever helps you feel in control and secure, even for a moment. It's happening in environments that care more about output than what's actually going on with people.

One pattern I've seen again and again is the need for control. Many CEOs and upper management figures carry the belief that their authority in business should extend to every area of life. But addiction doesn't respect power. It defies control. And that's terrifying for someone who's used to calling the shots.

The paradox is that the way out of addiction begins not with a tighter grip, but with surrender. Only by admitting you can't control everything do you begin to reclaim the parts of your life that truly matter.

Addiction among executives often hides in plain sight. It's not always the stereotypical image of someone drinking in secret or disappearing on benders. Sometimes it's the CEO who hasn't taken a day off in years. The VP who can't sleep without a drink. The founder who clings to work because everything at home is falling apart, and holding the company together feels like the only thing keeping his life from collapsing. The dysfunction is masked as dedication.

These environments praise output, not honesty. Vulnerability is often viewed as weakness, not wisdom. So when leaders begin to unravel, the culture around them usually encourages more of the same: more hustle, more pressure, more escape.

Even well-known leaders have walked this path. One powerful example is Michael Dadashi, the CEO and founder of MHD Enterprises and Infinite Recovery. In 2009, Michael was at rock bottom, struggling with heroin and alcohol addiction, facing the wreckage of his personal and professional life, and trying to figure out what came next. He made the difficult decision to get sober, not knowing where it would lead, only that he couldn't keep going the way he was.

In early recovery, he didn't have much. But he had something that mattered: a new sense of purpose and a willingness to start over. Michael began rebuilding his life and started an electronics recycling company called MHD Enterprises. He made a bold decision to hire others in recovery. People who, like him, just needed someone to believe in them. Over time, that personal mission grew into a multimillion-dollar company.

Years later, he founded Infinite Recovery, a treatment center designed to help others find the freedom he fought for. The journey taught him discipline, humility, and how to lead with empathy. He learned to own his story, take risks, and build something of substance. And eventually, those risks paid off in both business and purpose.

His story reflects a belief he's lived out through both of his companies: your past doesn't define you. What matters is what you choose to do with it.

Michael's story proves that recovery can be the beginning of a deeper kind of leadership. One shaped by humility, resilience, and purpose. Sobriety made him a better leader.

His experience reveals a deeper truth: there's something powerful that happens when an executive confronts addiction head-on. They start leading from a place of honesty. They start creating cultures where truth is valued over performance. And often, their companies thrive in deeper ways. Not just in revenue, but in loyalty, creativity, and connection.

I've worked with leaders who've come out on the other side of addiction with more clarity, empathy, and purpose than ever before. They didn't lose their edge, they sharpened it. When you've faced your own demons and lived to tell the story, there's a different kind of confidence that emerges. It's not bravado. It's not fake positivity. It's real, grounded strength rooted in knowing exactly who you are.

They also become better at supporting others. Once you've experienced the weight of hiding and the relief of getting honest, you stop pretending everything's fine. You stop judging others who struggle. You become the kind of leader people trust.

From Denial to Awareness

Denial is easier when you're "high-functioning." You're still closing deals. You're still getting applause. No one wants to look in the mirror and say, "I'm in trouble." Admitting that feels like admitting weakness, and weakness is the one thing you believe you're not allowed to show. Plus, when things look good on paper, money's coming in, your name carries weight, and people are looking to you for answers, it can feel like you've got the world in the palm of your hands. Why stop to question it when everyone else sees a success story?

Under the surface, something is starting to crack. It's like a small chip in your windshield, barely noticeable at first, but with time, pressure, cold weather and neglect, it spreads. Slowly, steadily, it takes over your view. You're drinking or using to get through the day, not just to celebrate. You're disengaged from family, but obsessed with work. You feel anxious or numb almost all the time. You can't imagine doing this for another five years with the way things are going. You stop enjoying the wins. You start dreading Monday mornings. Your phone becomes both a lifeline and a leash. You don't recognize the person you see in photos anymore, and the smile you wear in public doesn't match what you feel inside.

Sometimes it's not even a dramatic fall that wakes you up. Sometimes it's something small. A moment with your kid you're too tired to enjoy, or a conversation with your spouse where you realize you weren't really listening. It's that ache in your gut when you realize the thing you built is costing you the people you built it for.

I've seen executives take that first step when a friend spoke up, when a spouse gave an ultimatum, or when they did something that finally scared them. It's not always dramatic, either. Sometimes it's just a quiet truth that you can't ignore anymore.

No one can make you stop. You have to want it. You have to decide.

Here are some of the real drivers I've seen, and felt:

Chronic Stress & Overdrive
The grind never stops. There's always another meeting, another fire, another competitor. "Unplugging" is for people with less responsibility.

Isolation at the Top
You can't just call a friend and say, "I think I'm falling apart." You're the one others lean on. You're expected to keep it together. Always.

Performance-Based Identity
When your sense of worth is built on output and external validation, any crack in the armor feels like collapse. The default reaction is to double down, not ask for help.

Unresolved Past
A surprising number of executives are running from something, childhood trauma, abuse, insecurity. Their drive isn't purely ambition, it's escape.

Culture of Excess

The environment itself becomes a drug. Status signals safety. Luxury justifies indulgence. And with enough success, the rules start to feel optional.

Telling the Truth Strategically

You don't need to go on social media and announce you're struggling. But you do need a plan. Silence can be a shield for a while, but eventually, it becomes a weight. Secrets grow heavy. In the executive world, when you carry that kind of hidden pain, it doesn't stay hidden for long. It shows up in decisions, in demeanor, and in the form of distractions. That's why stepping forward with honesty, even quietly, is one of the most powerful moves you can make.

I coach executives on how to approach these conversations in a way that's thoughtful, clear, and grounded in real life. Not everyone needs to know everything. But someone does. Whether it's a trusted mentor, a close colleague, or a board member, opening up to the right person matters. These conversations don't have to be dramatic or overly detailed. They just need to be honest and real.

It might sound like: "I'm working through some personal challenges and making changes to take care of my health. I may need to adjust some things in my schedule or delegate more in the coming weeks. I'm committed to my role and the team, and I'm also committed to making sure I show up the right way."

That kind of honesty earns respect. More often than not, it also opens doors for others to be honest, too. Vulnerability, especially from leaders, has a ripple effect. It creates space for truth. It fosters trust. It signals strength, not weakness.

Telling the truth is an act of leadership. It shows you're not just performing. You're leading from a place of wholeness, not image. In a culture that often rewards performance over presence, that's a rare and powerful thing.

Recovery as Leadership

Recovery makes you honest. And honest leaders are rare.

When you've faced your own stuff, the habits, the pressure, the pain, you stop leading from fear or image. You start leading in a way that's honest and grounded. You make clearer choices. You stop chasing approval. You stop avoiding the hard conversations.

I've seen leaders earn more respect in recovery than they ever did chasing performance, not just because they had the courage to stop hiding, but because people saw their boldness, their toughness, their honesty, and because they became a better version of themselves.

When You See It in Someone Else

Sometimes, the first step toward change doesn't start with the person struggling, it starts with someone around them who cares enough to notice. You can usually tell when something's off. They seem different. Distracted. Maybe they're drinking more, or you've seen them repeatedly go too far and drink in excess. They're not themselves lately.

The hardest part isn't seeing it. It's deciding what to do about it.

Most people stay silent. They don't want to upset someone or offend anyone. They assume it's not their place. Or they tell themselves, "They've got it under control." But silence can be dangerous. When no one says anything, the person struggling stays stuck in the illusion that everything's fine, or at least that no one notices.

You don't have to be a therapist. You don't have to fix their problem. You can be a mirror, though. A trusted voice that says, "Hey, I've noticed you haven't been yourself lately. I care about you. If you ever want to talk, I'm here."

These conversations are uncomfortable, but they're also powerful. They don't have to be dramatic. In fact, the best ones are often quiet, simple, and rooted in genuine care.

You might say something like:

- "I've seen a few things lately that concern me. I'm not judging. I'm just here if you want to talk."
- "You don't have to explain anything, but I want you to know you're not alone."
- "I've been through tough seasons too, and if you ever want to share what's going on, I've got you."

That said, no one can force someone else to change. Recovery is a personal decision. But you can ask thoughtful questions that invite reflection and personal responsibility. Especially questions that go deeper than behavior and tap into identity, values, and character.

Questions like:

- "Is this who you want to be known as?"
- "Are your actions today aligned with the kind of person and leader you want to be?"
- "What kind of legacy are you building, and is this part of it?"
- "If someone you respect were watching you, would you feel proud of your behavior?"
- "What are you afraid might happen if you got honest about what's really going on?"

These questions are not judgmental ones. They actually will create an internal conversation that can be hard to ignore once it starts.

If the situation feels more serious, or if the person isn't responding and their behavior is impacting others, you may need to take the concern to someone in a position of authority.

That could mean quietly speaking to a manager, HR partner, or executive leader you trust. You don't need to come with accusations. Just express concern, share specific observations, and let them decide how to follow up. Something like, "I'm not sure what's going on, but I've noticed a few things that worry me, and I think it's worth someone checking in."

Leadership can then step in with more structure and resources, often in a way that protects the individual while also protecting the team and the company.

Sometimes a simple moment of honesty plants the seed. It might not change things overnight, but it opens the door. In a culture where silence is the default, even one real conversation can make a difference.

If you see someone struggling, don't ignore it. Say something. Not to shame them. Not to fix them. But to remind them that they're not invisible and they don't have to go through it alone.

Building a Recovery-Friendly Life

Sobriety or healing isn't a finish line. It's a lifestyle.

Executives who thrive in recovery learn to: Set clear boundaries (including with their calendar), Build routines that reduce chaos and temptation, Rethink success, from "more" to "meaning," and surround themselves with people who tell the truth, not just say "yes."

There are also executive-level recovery groups and accountability circles that offer peer support without judgment. For some leaders, these become lifelines.

Where Leadership Meets Real Life

Organizations that want to keep good people and help them heal need to rethink what strength really looks like. It's not about hiding pain. It's about having the courage to face it, and the wisdom to get help.

I work directly with executives who are ready to confront addiction in a way that fits the realities of their lives. Quietly.

Privately. With the kind of support that understands the weight of leadership.

For many high-performing leaders, asking for help feels risky. They don't want to be seen in a group setting. They're not ready to be public about what they're facing. They want discretion, privacy, and a path that respects who they are, and what they're responsible for. That's what I offer.

The goal is simple: to help people take back control of their lives and grow to become the best version of themselves.

Here are a few ways I support leaders as they begin that process and build lives that reflect who they truly want to be.

1:1 Coaching

Private coaching focused on recovery from addiction. We talk openly about habits, pressure, identity, and what it looks like to actually thrive. It's private, focused, and completely tailored to where you are.

Small Group or Team Coaching

For leadership teams or peer groups who want to build trust, alignment, and emotional resilience.

These sessions focus on:

- *Foundational Principles* — Clarifying what your organization truly stands for. We explore core values, non-negotiables, and the culture you're committed to building.
- *Character* — Looking at how personal integrity and emotional awareness shape leadership. We talk about

accountability, honesty, and what it means to show up with consistency.

- *Alignment* — Making sure individuals are in sync with the team and the mission. Misalignment is often where burnout and dysfunction begin.
- *Assignment* — Helping each person understand their unique role and contribution. This is about purpose, not just job titles.
- *Adjustment* — Being honest about what needs to change, personally and professionally, to move forward in a healthier, more sustainable way.

These conversations are raw, real, and rooted in experience. We talk about what's hard, what's working, and what's getting in the way. This is team development with depth, not another trust fall or offsite.

For more information about my coaching programs, you can go to my website, JoeyMCoaching.com

Final Reflection: You're Not Alone, and You're Not Done

Healing shouldn't require humiliation. Recovery shouldn't feel like a step down. The goal is to help executives rise, not just back to their old performance, but into a better version of themselves and also better in their leadership roles.

If you're in a leadership role and struggling, you're not the only one. A lot of people won't say it out loud, but that doesn't mean it's not happening.

Addiction, burnout, and emotional overload don't care how successful you are. They don't care about your title, your income, or your reputation. They show up anyway.

And when they do, most people stay quiet. Especially in leadership. Because being honest feels risky. Like failure. Like weakness.

But here's the truth: silence doesn't protect you. It just delays the cost.

You don't need to announce it to the world. You don't need to blow up your life overnight. But at some point, you have to tell the truth—to yourself, and to someone who can help. That's where it starts.

I know, because I lived it.

I was running a business. Chasing goals. Taking care of everyone else. That's where all my energy went. I didn't think I had time to deal with the deeper stuff. So I didn't.

I drank to not feel.

Eventually, my health gave me an ultimatum: keep going the way I was—or die.

I chose to take a new path. The path of recovery.

And that changed my life.

Today, I'm finishing my psychology degree. I'm writing this book. I'm a coach. And I'm a full-time girl dad to an incredibly smart, creative, and strong daughter for whom I get to show up every day.

My life isn't perfect. There are still hard moments. But I'm here for them now. I don't numb. I don't run. I don't lie about how I'm doing.

No matter how hard a day gets, I don't want the old life back. Not for a second.

My worst day sober is still better than my best day drunk.

I used to wear the mask of success to hide the pain.

I don't do that anymore.

*My worst day sober
is still better than
my best day drunk.*

Acknowledgments

First and above all, I want to thank **God**. Without His grace, mercy, and faithfulness, I wouldn't be here to write these words. He carried me through the darkest seasons, gave me strength when I had none, and offered forgiveness I didn't deserve. Every blessing in my life is a testament to His goodness. This book is ultimately for His glory, and I pray it points others toward Him.

To my wife, **Brandy**—thank you for standing beside me in the hardest moments and believing in the man I could become, even when I couldn't see him myself. Your strength, patience, and love are pillars in my life. You've been my steady through every storm—fierce, loyal, and all-in. I'm better because of you. I love you more than words will ever capture.

To my mom, **Debbie**—thank you for introducing me to Jesus early on. You were the first to show me what faith looked like, and those roots stayed with me, even when I drifted. Thank you for loving me through every season, through every mistake.

You never gave up on me, no matter how far I fell, and I'm forever grateful for that.

To my coach, **Alex Molden**—thank you for being so much more than a coach. Your wisdom, honesty, and unwavering commitment to asking the right questions helped me truly discover who I am and who I want to be. Your example of character, integrity, and faith continues to shape me. I'm beyond grateful for your friendship and guidance.

Grant, my counselor from Hazelden—thank you for helping me find steady ground when everything felt shaky. Your guidance in those early days of sobriety was crucial. I am forever grateful.

To **Dr. Schlansky**—thank you for your expert care, honesty, and compassion as my liver specialist. You didn't sugarcoat the truth—you told me that if I didn't quit, I would die. That conversation changed everything. You scared it out of me, and I thank God for that. Everything you said would happen, as long as I did my part, has happened. I can't thank you enough for your role in saving my life.

To **Dr. Wendland**, my primary care doctor—thank you for being a steady presence through so many chapters of this journey. Your support has meant more than I can say.

To **Dr. Diller** and **Dr. Inscore**—thank you both for your surgical care, skill, and attention along the way. I'm grateful for the part you played in helping restore my health.

To all the **nurses, ultrasound staff,** and **paracentesis teams**— thank you for your kindness, professionalism, and care during some of the most vulnerable moments. Your work made a difficult time more bearable, and I'm deeply grateful.

To **Pastor Brett, Pastor James,** and my home church, **Athey Creek**—thank you for always welcoming me, encouraging me, and reminding me that God's love and grace, through His Son, aren't something I could ever earn, but a gift freely given.

To my health coach, **Alicia**—thank you for helping me rebuild from the inside out.

To **Dan Janal**—this book wouldn't have happened without you. Thank you for your expert guidance, encouragement, and patience in helping me bring this story to life.

Sai and **Bill**—thank you for always being there. Your friendship, honesty, and loyalty through every season have meant the world to me.

To **Johnathan, Bonny,** and **Kevin** from AA—thank you for your friendship in the early days of sobriety, and for your continued support. I'm deeply thankful for each of you.

To my brother, **Dave Jr.,** I'm proud of you. Keep going.

To anyone I may have missed—know that you're part of this, too. Thank you for standing by me.

And to everyone I've thanked here: I hope this book makes you proud.

Would Your School, Group, or Business Benefit from Hearing Joey's Message?

Joey McCollum is passionate about helping others move from surviving to thriving. Whether through speaking, workshops, or one-on-one coaching, he brings honesty, humor, and hard-won insight to the conversation.

If you'd like to invite Joey to speak to your group, appear on your podcast, or work with you individually, he'd love to hear from you.

Visit **joeymccollum.com** for contact details, resources, and upcoming events.

About the Author

Joey McCollum is a husband, father, and former athlete who knows firsthand the struggle of addiction and the hard-won freedom on the other side. After a promising sports career was cut short, he spent years running from pain and numbing himself with alcohol, until a doctor's blunt warning forced him to confront the truth: "If you don't quit drinking, you will die." That moment was the start of a messy, difficult, but ultimately life-changing journey into sobriety and healing.

Today, Joey is committed to living with integrity, purpose, and faith. He is open about the challenges he's faced, from losing his identity as an athlete to rebuilding his life in recovery. A devoted father, he went back to college after 24 years to finish his degree in psychology, determined to understand the roots of addiction and help others find freedom. His mission is to show that it's never too late to change, no matter how far you've fallen.

Through writing, coaching, and speaking, Joey shares his story to offer hope to those stuck in cycles of addiction, shame, or self-doubt. He believes in honesty over image, grace over guilt, and faith as the foundation for lasting change. He lives in Oregon with his family, where he continues to grow, heal, and remind others—and himself—that the words **I don't do that anymore** can be the start of everything new.